The
Essential
Guide to
Bipolar
Disorder

Robert Duffy Series Editor

Published in Great Britain in 2017 by
need2know
Remus House
Coltsfoot Drive
Peterborough
PE2 9BF
Telephone 01733 898103
www.need2knowbooks.co.uk

Contents

Introduction

O riginally referred to as 'manic depression,' bipolar disorder is a common oondition which affects about 1 per cent of adults. That amounts to around 12 million people in the US, 2.4 million in the UK and 254 million people internationally. It's characterised by severe mood swings which can usually last a few weeks but can last for several months.

In most cases, bipolar disorder starts between the ages of 15 and 19, and very rarely after the age of 40. Whereas 'unipolar' depression also known as major depressive disorder - more commonly affects women, bipolar affects all sexes equally.

Each person's experience of illnesses is unique and individual to them, but moods will generally swing between extreme highs - often referred to as 'manic' episodes, as suggested by its original name - where the sufferer will experience euphoria, limitless energy and a great sense of supreme confidence; and devastating low or 'depressive' moods, featuring feelings of intense despair and unhappiness. People with this condition can also experience a 'mixed state' which combines features of the two extremes. For example, they may experience the despair of a depressed mood, while also struggling with the restlessness of a manic episode. The condition can even cause warped, strange thinking and hallucinations, which may lead to confusion over what is happening, and why it's happening to you.

Living with bipolar can be a confusing, frightening experience, especially when you are yet to receive a diagnosis and/or treatment. Those with the disorder will find themselves shifting constantly between periods where they feel unstoppable and have no real desire to eat or sleep, and periods of miserable, dark moods. Those who care about you may find themselves deeply concerned for your welfare.

It's not all bad news, though! Over the last few decades, treatment for bipolar disorder has been greatly improved. Following diagnosis, those with the disorder are likely to receive treatment in the form of a large combination of different drugs, which will include an antidepressant to combat low moods, a mood stabiliser (lithium, for example) and sometimes other medications depending on the individual case. In many cases, psychiatrists will also recommend therapy, such as cognitive behavioural therapy (CBT).

It is incredibly important that those with bipolar receive a professional diagnosis as early in the development of the condition as possible, as this will give the best chance of successful treatment and positive long-term outcomes. It's believed that it is generally significantly easier to successfully treat someone who has had less than three episodes. This is something we will discuss further in Chapter Five: Getting a Diagnosis.

Regardless of diagnoses, learning to listen to your mind and body and take the best possible care of yourself is vital in managing your own mental and physical health. This behaviour is known as 'self-care,' and is an incredibly important tool when it comes to managing bipolar disorder. Your condition can be improved to an amazing degree if you learn to recognise what triggers your high and low moods, and to give yourself what you need in terms of diet, stress management, sleep and exercise.

The aim of this book is to help the reader identify whether they could possibly be living with bipolar disorder, and to understand the types of help that's available to you and your loved ones in the event of a diagnosis. We will explain exactly what will happen if you receive a professional diagnosis, and why it's so important that you do seek a professional diagnosis if you believe you have bipolar disorder. We'll also explain what sort of mental health professionals are available to support and assist you, and which options are available for treatment, both on the NHS and through private care.

We also hope to help you understand the causes of bipolar disorder, how it manifests itself and what impact this will have on your everyday life, as well as what your friends and family will need to know in order to help you, and what support will be available for them.

Above all else, this book hopes to help you understand that being diagnosed with bipolar disorder is not the end of the world. Many of those living with bipolar go on to lead satisfying, happy lives so long as they look after themselves to the best of their ability and receive all the treatment they need. The first step towards living your content, healthy life is to arm yourself with all of the information you will need, and this book is a great place to start.

As a final note, we wish to thank everyone who helped to create this book by openly and bravely describing their own experiences with bipolar disorder. Despite the many difficulties posed by the condition, these people are living illustrations of how - with the right treatment and information - those with bipolar disorder can still live their best lives.

Please note:

This book is intended only to provide general information about bipolar disorder, and is by no means to be used as a replacement for professional medical advice. If you suspect you may be suffering from bipolar disorder, please contact your GP as soon as possible.

The names of some of the case studies cited in this text have been changed.

1

What is Bipolar Disorder?

Everyone experiences mood swings to a certain extent. We can be enthusiastic and happy about our lives one day, and inconsolably miserable the next. This is just what it is to experience the broad spectrum of moods and emotions that make up the human experience. For some, however, these mood swings are far more severe and can have devastating effects on their day-to-day lives. These individuals may find themselves swinging between being incredibly animated, confident and happy, and being sad, tired and depressed.

In the past, people who suffered from these sorts of mood swings were diagnosed with a condition called 'manic depression.' This continued right up until 1980, when it was renamed 'bipolar disorder' by the American Psychiatric Association (APA) to reflect the dual nature or 'bi-polarity' of the condition. Some believe the original name describes the condition's manic highs and depressive lows more accurately, while others suggest that 'multi-polar disorder' would be a better name as it highlights that the condition involves more than two moods.

> 'Bipolar disorder is a serious mental health problem involving extreme swings of mood (highs and lows).'
>
> MDF: the BiPolar Organisation

While we obviously need some sort of name by which to address bipolar disorder, it's important to remember that that's all it is: a name. Some people find the use of labels when describing someone's life experiences, mental and physical health challenges and personality to be unhelpful as it can lead people to forget that each of these factors is unique to the person experiencing them. Some experts have taken to referring to bipolar as a 'spectrum disorder' as the impact it has on each person's life is as individual as the people themselves. Symptoms range broadly from very mild to very severe, which is why it's important that you find the treatment that's right for you.

Your rights as a patient

Your treatment and care should take into account your personal needs and preferences, and you have the right to be fully informed and to make decisions in partnership with your healthcare team. To help with this, your healthcare team should give you information you can understand and that is relevant to your circumstances. All healthcare professionals should treat you with respect, sensitivity and understanding and explain bipolar disorder and the treatments for it simply and clearly.

According to the NICE (National Institute for Health and Clinical Excellence), this is the treatment you should expect from your healthcare professionals. It is incredibly important that you and the people around you are aware of all the types of treatment you are entitled to on receiving a diagnosis. This is especially important when it comes to bipolar disorder, as the NHS provision for the condition varies from place to place, even within the UK.

Getting access to talking therapies

In order to access talking therapies through the NHS, you need to first talk to your GP. If they believe you would benefit from a talking therapy, they'll refer you to a therapist trained in family-focused therapy, CBT or counselling (these different methods will be discussed in greater detail in Chapter Seven: Talking Therapies), such as a nurse, psychiatrist, social worker or psychologist.

Any type of talking therapy should be provided by a highly-trained, skilled practitioner. Unfortunately however, as a result of funding cuts to the NHS, it is not uncommon for people with very limited training to offer CBT, which is not always helpful. If you feel this is the case and are unhappy with the treatment you receive, do not hesitate to raise the issue with your therapist. It is your well-being at stake here, and you have every right to receive proper treatment from a professional.

Try not to be tempted to be over-polite or to spare someone's feelings (within reason!) on this matter. Treatment with the NHS can be relatively hit-and-miss, and often the quality of treatment you receive will depend on where you live, with certain areas receiving better services than others. For this reason, if you can afford it, it can be a good idea to consider looking into private treatment.

Along with the higher likelihood of receiving proper treatment, private therapists are often able to offer far more sessions than those who work through the NHS. Research has found that even with treatments such as CBT which are typically time-limited, longer periods of therapy with the option of follow-up sessions are generally significantly more helpful than the six sessions you will be offered through the NHS.

Keep in mind, however, that psychotherapy is currently an unregulated industry. While the government is trying to change this, there are countless psychotherapists and counsellors practising right now who have very questionable skill levels and training. If you are looking for a therapist to treat you privately, be sure to search through the main governing bodies: the UKCP (psychotherapy), BABCP (CBT therapists) and BACP (counsellors).

What is a Mood Disorder?

'Mood disorder' is the name given to a group of diagnoses by the manual used by mental health professionals such as psychiatrists to diagnose mental illnesses, known as the Diagnostic and Statistical Manual of Mental Disorders (DSM-IV). These are disorders wherein the patient's mood is the primary underlying feature, and include unipolar depression (major depressive disorder), bipolar disorder (manic-depressive disorder) and chronic minor depression (dysthymia).

Bipolar disorder is set apart from the other two conditions listed here by its shift between two distinct moods. According to Jan Scott, in her book *Overcoming Mood Swings: A Self-Help Guide Using Cognitive Behavioral Techniques* (see book list), problematic mood swings – as opposed to normal changes in mood – share some or all of these characteristics. These mood swings often share some or all of the following characteristics:

- Unpredictable: The individual's mood fluctuates often, but with no obvious cause.

- Extreme: The individual always experiences moods as extreme highs or lows.

- Extensive: The moods experienced by the individual will last a long time.

- Disruptive: They may cause considerable issues in the lives of the patient, their friends and their family.

- Accompanied: Mood swings often come hand-in-hand with associated changes in the individual's behaviour, biological systems and thoughts.

- Excessive: The mood swings happen very frequently and over a large number of years.

- Uncontrollable: The individual sometimes has no control over their emotional responses to certain events, and as a result their reactions often appear inappropriate.

Bipolar disorder shares a number of symptoms with other conditions, but is still its own distinct condition. For example, people suffering from generalised anxiety disorder (GAD) will find themselves worrying immoderately and almost constantly about issues that others will believe are insignificant or unlikely to happen. This is a condition which mostly affects women, and overall impacts around 3-4% of the population of the US and many other Western countries. It's also connected with panic attacks, which are unpredictable, sudden episodes of severe anxiety and fear, often combined with a rapid heartbeat, choking sensations and shortness of breath.

Stress is a problem which impacts everyone at some time or another, while chronic stress is one that affects people who work under a great amount of pressure and for long hours. If it isn't treated correctly, frequent stress can cause a whole array of mental and physical problems including ulcers, depression, breakdown, burnout, anxiety and high blood pressure.

Post-traumatic stress disorder (PTSD) is a separate condition which is caused by extremely disturbing experiences or long periods of these experiences. The condition is frequently associated with veterans dealing with traumatic experiences of war, but it can be experienced by anyone who has survived or witnessed a traumatic event. Symptoms of PTSD include nightmares, hallucinations and flashbacks (where the traumatic event is relived through the individual's memories).

Types of Bipolar Disorder

There are two primary types of bipolar disorder described in the DSM-IV. These ideas will be explored in closer detail later in the book.

Bipolar I

Bipolar I is the diagnosis given to individuals who have experienced a minimum of one manic episode, lasting for at least one week, in their lifetime. Whereas most people diagnosed with Bipolar I will have periods of both depression and mania, some will only experience manic episodes. It's believed that about 1% of the population will develop this condition at some stage.

Bipolar II

In order to be diagnosed with Bipolar II, the individual needs to have experienced at least one episode of severe depression, with manic episodes which are significantly milder (hypomania). This condition is more common, affecting somewhere between 4-5% of the population at some point in their lives. The diagram on the following page, originally printed in Jan Scott's *Overcoming Mood Swings*, makes clear how Bipolar I and II differ, as well as the difference between them and purely depressive mood disorders.

We'll look at depressive episodes in greater detail in the next chapter.

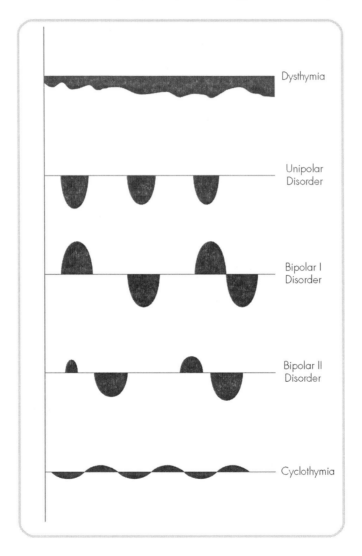

Table from *Overcoming Mood Swings* by Jan Scott (Constable & Robinson, London, 2000) by kind permission of the publishers.

Rapid Cycling

If you have more than 4 mood swings over the space of 12 months, this is known as rapid cycling. Rapid cycling affects individuals with Bipolar I and Bipolar II alike, impacting around 10% of people with bipolar disorder.

Cyclothymia

Cyclothymia is a term used for a milder form of bipolar disorder, where the individual has manic and depressive symptoms for over two years, but nothing severe enough to merit a diagnosis of bipolar disorder. The condition is associated with brief, frequent periods of depression and hypomanic symptoms, punctuated by periods of stability. In some cases, an individual with cyclothymia may experience mood swings which grow increasingly severe until they are eventually diagnosed with Bipolar I or II.

The complex nature of moods and emotions means that it can often be difficult to diagnose someone with cyclothymia, as some people are simply more moody or emotional than others. The idea of what is 'normal' and what is a mental illness varies to an amazing degree between countries and cultures, so the diagnosis of cyclothymia is an ongoing argument between many mental health experts. What some people may consider to be suspicious or worrying, others may simply believe to be 'flamboyant'.

The difference between mania and hypomania

(T)he mood is elevated or irritable to a degree that is definitely abnormal for the individual concerned and sustained for at least four consecutive days.

This is the description of hympomania given by the World Health Organisation (WHO). Hypomania is occasionally branded 'mania lite' as a great number of its symptoms are simply less-extreme versions of symptoms belonging to full-blown mania. The condition is a grey area to a certain degree, with experts believing it may often be diagnosed rather than mania due to its sounding more acceptable.

The following is a list of hypomanic symptoms, which you may notice appear very similar to many manic symptoms:

- Feelings of improved self-esteem with exceptionally high confidence
- Becoming more talkative than usual
- Feeling distractable and unable to concentrate on one activity
- Interest in questionable activities with less consideration for the consequences
- Increased energy levels and activity
- Higher levels of creativity and productivity
- Feeling more sociable than usual, both with friends and strangers
- Blissful, excited moods which can last for a number of days before changing to impatience, rage or irritability
- Constantly working towards certain goals
- Racing thoughts and seemingly unlimited supply of ideas
- Reduced need for sleep

Importantly, hypomania is fairly common even among those without bipolar disorder. If you consider your friends and coworkers, it is likely that more than one of them will exhibit some of these symptoms at times. Some people are very friendly and full of energy most of the time, and that's fine. It only becomes a problem when these energetic periods come with episodes of excessively high or low moods, which interfere with their day to day lives.

How Does Someone Usually Get Diagnosed?

In most cases people with bipolar will experience at least one depressive episode before experiencing a manic one. This can make it very challenging for doctors to correctly diagnose the condition initially, which is why bipolar disorder is often misdiagnosed at first. In many cases, your condition will only be recognised as bipolar following a severe manic episode - particularly one which causes issues with police or lands the patient in hospital.

All of this means it's also very unlikely that your GP will be willing or able to diagnose you with bipolar disorder. They will either give you a misdiagnosis, or will refer you to a psychiatrist who will be able to give you a more accurate diagnosis. If it is suspected that you are suffering from bipolar, you will be given an assessment. This will involve a series of relevant questions which will help decide your diagnosis and potential treatments.

The questions will concern events and emotions you may have experienced prior to developing symptoms of bipolar, whether you have considered hurting yourself or others and whether any other members of your family live with the condition. Some psychiatrists will also want to talk to a family member, but will ask for your permission before doing so.

We'll talk more about getting the right diagnosis in Chapter 5.

Why is bipolar misdiagnosed?

It has been estimated that almost 70% of patients with bipolar disorder initially receive the wrong diagnosis, with an average delay of eight years before the correct diagnosis is made. Obviously, this is far from an ideal scenario. The main misdiagnosis for those with bipolar disorder is major depression, though psychiatrists often mistake bipolar symptoms for schizophrenia in cases where the patient experiences psychotic symptoms.

Research has found that around 33% of those diagnosed with major depression are actually experiencing bipolar. Researchers from the University of Texas Health Science Center have suggested psychiatrists should consider five main characteristics to determine whether a patient's 'depression' is in fact bipolar disorder. These characteristics include…

- A family history of mania
- Development of initial psychiatric symptoms under the age of 30
- Mixed states in which symptoms of both depression and mania have occurred together
- Development of extreme mood swings
- Experience of at least 2 mood episodes in the past

Further studies suggest that the amount of patients to receive an incorrect diagnosis initially may be a lower 40%, with these patients still having to wait a number of years for the proper diagnosis.

The danger of misdiagnosis is that patients who are misdiagnosed with major depression are often prescribed antidepressants. In those with bipolar disorder, taking antidepressants without an additional mood stabiliser can often cause the patient to experience a manic episode.

Symptoms of Depression and Mania

Bipolar disorder is associated with drastic shifts between two main states: highs, or manic episodes, and lows, or depressive episodes. The length of time each mood can last varies drastically from individual to individual, or from year to year. Some people experience states lasting months, weeks or days, while others can experience several mood swings in the space of a day.

As with most illnesses, the nature of your symptoms will be entirely unique to you, but there are some symptoms which are more common than others. This is a guide to some of the most common symptoms of bipolar disorder, and how you might deal with them.

Depression

There's a big difference between feeling a little down in the mouth or fed up - which everyone experiences now and then - and clinical depression, which is a much more serious condition and lasts a great deal longer. Individuals who suffer from this type of depression may deal with a combination of the following symptoms:

- Persistent feelings of unhappiness
- A loss of interest in former passions, and an inability to enjoy them
- Loss of self-confidence
- Suicidal and otherwise negative thoughts
- Reduced weight and appetite
- Exhaustion
- Feelings of isolation and avoidance
- Reduced sex drive
- Difficulty sleeping
- Lack of decisiveness and concentration

- Feelings of incompetence, hopelessness and uselessness
- Feelings of unrest, irritation and restlessness
- Unexplained desire to cry

Mania

As with depression, it's important to distinguish between feeling a bit agitated or hyperactive, and 'mania', which is more severe and often escalates. People experiencing manic episodes commonly experience:

- Feelings of enthusiasm and happiness
- Feelings of importance
- Constant switching from one idea to the next
- Inability or unwillingness to sleep
- Compulsion to make impractical and grandiose plans
- Strange behaviour
- Making hasty, odd decisions with little to no consideration of consequences
- Finding faults and being over-familiar with others
- Lack of inhibitions
- Reckless spending
- Talking unusually quickly
- Desire to move and act very quickly
- Increased sex drive
- High amounts of energy
- Unusual amounts of thrilling, new ideas
- Irritation when others don't share your positive point of view

Mixed States

Some individuals diagnosed with bipolar disorder may experience a 'mixed state,' with symptoms of both depression and mania at the same time. For example, they may have a depressed mood but still struggle with the hyperactivity and restlessness of mania. Mixed states are very common indeed in people with bipolar, with an estimated two-thirds experiencing at least one mixed episode at one stage.

A mixed state may not sound any more serious than other bipolar symptoms, but can actually become a very dangerous combination of emotions. Unlike the two polar extremes, a mixed state may cause someone to have the suicidal thoughts they might have during a depressive episode, but also have the energy and drive to actually put those suicidal thoughts in motion. If you find yourself in this position, it is vital that you tell a mental health professional or GP so they can get you the help you need.

Psychotic Symptoms

If a manic or depressive episode becomes very acute, individuals may begin experiencing 'psychotic' symptoms. In the case of an episode of depression, you may begin to feel that you are the worst person on earth, that you are more guilty than anyone else or that you don't even exist. Meanwhile, in a manic episode, psychotic symptoms tend to manifest in the form of grandiose self-beliefs. Some people begin to believe that they are on the verge of bringing about world peace, or on a mission to save the world. Others believe that they have developed special skills or powers. In some cases, you may begin to hallucinate. This is where someone smells, sees, feels or hears something that isn't there.

Between Episodes

It was once believed that people with bipolar disorder returned to normal between their mood swings. However, it is now known that this is rarely the case. For many people with bipolar disorder, curved thinking and mild depressive symptoms may be experienced even when they feel 'better'. However, everyone's experiences of the condition are unique to them, and what you experience between highs and lows may well be different from what is described here.

Who Gets Bipolar Disorder?

Whereas conditions such as major depressive disorder are believed to affect some demographics more than others (in the case of unipolar depression, women are affected more often than men), bipolar disorder appears to affect women and men equally. Although there is some evidence that suggests an exception between the ages of 16 and 25 - where more men are affected than women - after the age of 26, it is mostly women who are diagnosed with the condition.

Mental health experts also believe that women generally experience more rapid cycles, with moods that change more frequently and a greater amount of mixed states.

On average, people are diagnosed with bipolar disorder around the age of 19. This age has dropped drastically from the average age of 32 in the mid-1990s. It is possible that this is due to an increase in drug abuse or in daily stressors, lifestyle factors which have been proven to trigger the condition and increase the severity of its symptoms. However, it's also possible that this is simply a result of an increased awareness of the illness.

Controversially, there has also been a massive increase in the US of childhood diagnoses of bipolar disorder, further decreasing the average age for diagnosis. For instance, the number of children in the US who have been diagnosed with bipolar disorder is now five times higher than it was eight years ago, with children as young as 2 or 3 years of age being diagnosed. Many mental health experts are reluctant to diagnose children with bipolar disorder, especially in the UK, and even more of these professionals are reluctant to offer the same powerful prescriptions given to children in the US.

Even among experts who don't support the belief that young children can have bipolar disorder, there are many who do believe that these children can exhibit certain behaviours which suggest they may develop bipolar disorder later in life. If this is the case, it should be possible for doctors and parents to keep an eye on the lifestyle and environment of an at-risk child in order to prevent the development of the condition later in life. We'll look at which lifestyle factors should be considered later in the book.

We do know that - while unusual - it is possible for an elderly person to be diagnosed with bipolar disorder, although the symptoms tend to be different in this demographic. In older patients, cycles are generally shorter and more severe. In most cases, those who are diagnosed at more than 50 years will have experienced either mania or depression earlier in their lives.

Co-Existing Illnesses and Conditions

Though the reasons for this link is unclear, we do know that people with bipolar disorder often find themselves engaging in substance abuse - misusing recreational drugs or alcohol, for example. At times, this will be due to reduced self-control during a manic episode, leading the person to drink more than they otherwise would or experiment with illegal drugs. Some individuals with bipolar will begin to self-medicate with drugs or alcohol, treating or masking their symptoms in a bid to feel better in the short-term.

It is important to note, however, that substance abuse can prolong or even trigger certain symptoms of bipolar disorder. Alcohol is a known depressant, while an extremely low mood is often experienced during the 'comedown' from many illegal drugs.

A number of anxiety disorders can also co-occur in people with bipolar, including social anxiety (extreme anxiety experienced in social situations) and post-traumatic stress disorder (PTSD). Overlapping symptoms like distractibility and restlessness also make it easy for bipolar disorder to co-occur with conditions like attention deficit hyperactivity disorder (ADHD).

It's incredibly important that people with bipolar monitor their mental and physical health carefully, as they are at a higher risk of suffering from migraines, diabetes, obesity, heart disease and thyroid disease, among other physical illnesses.

Summing Up

Once known as 'manic depression,' bipolar is a common mental health condition which is generally diagnosed in and around the teenage years. The condition gets its name from its characteristic swings between high moods, called mania, and lows, called depression.

While there are a range of common symptoms, the precise nature and length of these moods, the frequency of mood swings and conditions between moods are different for every individual.

Individuals with bipolar sometimes experience something called a 'mixed state,' which will feature symptoms of mania and depression at the same time. Patients may also develop psychotic symptoms including hallucinations and delusional thinking as a result of depressive or manic episodes becoming very severe.

The two most common forms of bipolar disorder are Bipolar I, characterised by a higher frequency of manic episodes, and Bipolar II, in which depressive episodes are more common. A less common diagnosis exists in the form of cyclothymia, a condition with similar but less severe mood swings. This condition often eventually develops into Bipolar I or II.

2

Depression (the lows)

Often, people with bipolar suggest that the early stages of a manic episode are actually quite enjoyable. They may enjoy feeling full of life, self-belief and confidence what make the world look beautiful and brimming with endless possibilities. Nobody would say the same about depression. The lower side of a bipolar mood swing tends to be an isolated, unhappy and dark place to inhabit. It's the polar opposite of the colourful world of mania.

Bipolar depression is not the same as unipolar depression. For example, people with bipolar disorder tend to sleep more, rather than less, during a depressive episode. All the same, the more common feelings, thoughts and general experience tend to be very similar. Mental health charities like MIND estimate that 25% of us will experience some type of mental distress at one point in our lives, with depression and anxiety the most common illnesses.

To an increasing degree, depression is becoming recognised as a basic part of the human condition, a darkness that develops often as a result of divorce, unemployment or bereavement. In some cases, it is argued that depression has become such a major part of our understanding of life that many overuse the term. Many people have taken to pathologising perfectly normal and healthy responses to negative stimuli, such as grief or sadness, even though these emotions will ease of their own accord.

Importantly, in bipolar and major depression, the experience is significantly worse than feeling a little down in the dumps. It's an illness that lasts much longer and makes it feel impossible to carry out simple tasks like relating to others, caring for children or working. In severe cases, depression can become a completely disabling sense of deep unhappiness or isolation.

Fortunately, doctors now have a greater understanding of depression than ever before, and we have a vast variety of powerful tools and treatments to help us get better.

Why do we get depressed?

Experts have loads of different ideas about why we get depressed and which treatments are the most effective. Some view it as a biological condition resulting from an imbalance of chemicals in our brain which control the way we feel, act and think, especially if the depression is part of bipolar disorder. Others insist that depression is entirely a result of our upbringing. These researchers argue that the condition is caused by problems which occurred in our youth and infancy, choosing to focus on the type of relationship we had with our parents rather than the physical structure of our brains.

For the most part, however, researchers in depression tend to agree that it is a complex combination of these two factors along with difficult events in later life and the ways in which we view these events that causes depression.

In this case, the experts refer to depression as a 'biophysical' disease - a condition which requires an understanding of the interaction between our bodily processes and biology, the circumstances we live in, our psychology, and the mental and bodily aspects of the illness.

'I just couldn't get out of bed. I had zero energy. Everything went dark. I was thinking to myself, "Why should I bother getting up? I can't solve any problems anyway, I'm incapable of doing anything."'

Former Norwegian Prime Minister, Kjell Magne Bondevik

Clinical psychologist Dorothy Rowe, one of the world's leading experts on depression, argues that we become depressed because of the way we view the world and, especially, the harsh and critical way we view ourselves. Her book, *Depression: The Way Out of Your Prison* (see book list), has brought comfort to thousands of readers since it was first published in 1983. In it, Rowe describes depression as 'a prison where you are both the suffering prisoner and the cruel jailer'.

Whatever your understanding of the condition, the way in which we think about ourselves and the events in our lives inarguably impact our likelihood to become depressed. If you are living with bipolar, having an understanding of 'depressive thinking' can be an invaluable tool when it comes to avoiding feeling down, and can also be helpful when you try to pull yourself out of a depressive episode. This is something we'll look at in greater detail later in the book.

What is depression?

Although it's only in the past few decades that we've began talking about depression as openly as we do, it certainly isn't a new condition. Depression is an illness which has afflicted man as far back as records go. Initially, though, the condition was named 'melancholia' by the ancient Greek doctor Hippocrates - a term which was also used later by Sigmund Freud.

Experts in mental health differentiate between mild or moderate depression and 'endogenous' depression, now known as major depression. This original term was used to signal that major depression generally stems from within, rather than as a result of an upsetting life event. Mild depression is distinguished from more severe types by the intensity of the symptoms. These were discussed in the previous chapter, but will be repeated here as a reminder:

- Persistent feelings of unhappiness
- Loss of interest and enjoyment from previous passions
- Loss of self-confidence
- Lack of decisiveness and concentration
- Reduced libido
- Feelings of avoidance and isolation

- Loss of weight and appetite
- Negative thoughts and suicidal ideation
- Feelings of incompetence, hopelessness and uselessness
- Annoyance, irritation and restlessness
- Unexplained desire to cry

Often the number of these symptoms you experience will signal the severity of your depression.

Depression is about much more than mood

Depression is about so much more than a simple low mood - though that's not to say that feeling low is any fun either! Depression also alters the way we think about things, our concentration, our libido, sleep and energy levels. All of this is explained in Professor Paul Gilbert's book, *Overcoming Depression: A Self-Help Guide Using Cognitive Behavioural Techniques*.

First of all, depression makes life difficult by draining any motivation we have to get stuff done. We begin to feel indifferent and exhausted, as though nothing could possibly be worth the effort it takes to get started. Every day - even one where you have no really challenging tasks - becomes an uphill battle, with simple tasks like getting up or taking a shower becoming completely impossible.

As if this isn't enough of a pain, we begin to lose the ability to experience any form of enjoyment. Life feels pointless and empty. And while we can no longer experience positive emotions, we often seem perfectly able to have negative feelings like irritation. Especially in men with depression, symptoms often manifest themselves in the form of annoyance, frustration and anger. We begin to lash out at the people around us, who are often our loved ones. We then feel guilty about our actions, leading us to spiral into an even deeper depression.

Depression can touch every part of our lives, affecting things like our relationships, thinking, bodies and behaviour. While it often seems as though we are unable to concentrate on anything, we also appear to be fully capable to concentrate on mistakes we have made and ways in which we have been wronged. People with depression often fall into the trap of becoming highly self-critical of themselves and those around them, labelling both themselves and the people they love as faulty, worthless, bad and inferior.

If you are suffering from depression, it is absolutely vital that you keep telling yourself that your condition does not make you a disappointment or a bad person. It is an illness, which is no more your fault than an allergy or asthma would be.

Feeling isolated and alone

One of the hardest parts of depression is the feeling that we are completely isolated from the world around us, and do not have the tools we need to communicate that we need help. In more severe cases, we may find that we are incapable even of reaching out and telling our closest family members and friends that we are struggling. We can see the world going on around us, but find it impossible to participate.

Of the many ironies depression brings with it, perhaps the greatest is that while struggling to ask for help, we often end up driving away the people we need. As with the other symptoms of bipolar, depressive episodes can be difficult for everyone affected, not just the person experiencing them. As a result, those who otherwise would be the most caring and considerate people you know may become unsympathetic, which can sometimes hurt more than the depression itself.

If you find yourself in this situation, it's important to keep in mind that the people around you are likely acting this way because they feel frustrated that they can't understand or help with the struggles you're going through. This is why books like this one should not only be read by those suffering from bipolar and depression, but by their friends and family as well.

As tempting as it might be to avoid annoying people by hiding in your bed and waiting for it to blow over, it's been found that one of the most effective ways of combatting depression is to surround yourself with other people (along with the proper talking therapies and medication, of course). Many of those suffering from bipolar and similar illnesses find online forums such as *Bipolar4all* to be a great way of finding and talking to people who understand exactly how you are feeling.

Depression and suicide

Suicide is a very real risk for anyone with a psychiatric illness, especially those with bipolar disorder. Studies have shown that those with bipolar are 15-20 times more likely to attempt suicide than the rest of the general population. Other research has found that somewhere between 25-50% of those with bipolar will attempt suicide at least once over the course of their lives. This is why it's so important that people with bipolar and their loved ones are aware of the risks and take them seriously. One of the most important ways to keep your loved ones safe is to learn the warning signs and triggers for suicide, and be aware of them.

If you suffer from bipolar disorder, the greatest risk of suicide occurs during mixed or depressive episodes. Experts warn that this risk is even higher when those who have been depressed are beginning to recover, when they suddenly have the energy that they require to commit suicide, but which they did not have when they were deeper in their depression.

Also note that if someone has even vaguely considered suicide in the past, they are more likely to attempt it when life becomes too much.

The following are a list of warning signs to consider if you believe that you (or someone you know) are at risk of suicide:

- Loss of self-esteem with feelings of loneliness, hopelessness and failure
- Feelings of worthlessness and uselessness
- Unexpectedly taking out life insurance or making a will
- Dramatic changes in behaviour, e.g. difficulty communicating or an unusual sense of calm
- Discussing suicide: There's a myth that those who talk about suicide will not go

through with it, but most people who commit suicide have discussed it with someone at some stage.

- Lack of self care, e.g. not caring about appearance, not eating properly
- Waking up early and other sleep problems

Why do people become suicidal?

They may less want to die than to escape an impossible situation, to relieve an unbearable state of mind, or to convey desperate feelings to others.

This, suggests MIND, is often the reason someone might decide to attempt suicide. The reasons someone with bipolar might attempt suicide tend to be the same as those that would cause anyone to end their life. Maybe you're experiencing a sudden personal crisis such as the end of a relationship, maybe you've run into a period of misfortune and trouble. Maybe you've simply been worn down by a lifetime of difficulty. Some professionals suggest that suicide may be a result of anger, often directed at oneself.

If you have bipolar disorder, any suicidal thoughts you have may also be contributed by delusional ideas caused by your condition. Some people find they hear voices that tell them to kill themselves. Others simply struggle to process their bipolar diagnosis and become overwhelmed.

In many cases, especially those involving young men, drug and alcohol abuse will increase the risk of suicide. Statistically, more men commit suicide than women, with four times more suicides being committed by men than women, and the highest suicide rate in the demographic of men between the ages of 15 and 44. Another major factor is unemployment, with suicide attempts occuring far more often in those who are unemployed than in those who have jobs.

Finally, according to the mental health charity MIND, certain individuals simply seem to have a desire to die, a feeling which grows more intense when they begin to feel hopeless

about the future. When people reach this point, suicide can often appear to be the only option remaining.

Most important of all is to keep in mind that even if someone is contemplating suicide as a cry for help rather than an end to their life, their life is still at risk and their suicidal ideation must be taken seriously. If you are in this situation, please talk to your mental health team, your GP, or a service like Samaritans who can be reached by phone on (08457 90 90 90) or by email at jo@samaritans.org.

Case study

Martin, 40, explains how painful bipolar depression can be and how severely it affects his relationships, even with the people closest to him. He also makes it clear how easily depressive thoughts can turn to suicide.

'For me it's not as you would imagine. Life can be great and everything is well – relationships, friends, everything, then somewhere deep inside is this blackness that takes over. You just don't want to be around those who love you and you end up hurting them. I found myself telling those close to me that all I wanted was to be under the ground.

'I would spend days in bed, not wash or eat, then I would get paranoid that everyone I knew hated me – and why wouldn't they? I hated me. The depression in my case could last for weeks, sometimes months, causing total destruction to relationships. We often think of depression as a feeling of sadness but with bipolar and my depression that sadness becomes more – it eats away at your very core and you have no control.

'It's like someone has taken away my ability to show emotion – you see things you love, like family, partner, friends, and you just don't want them there. I even asked my partner at the time to kill me and I've asked doctors to help me die.

That was my way of asking for help and it must be very hard for other people to understand, but to me it seemed like the best way.'

In an emergency

If you find yourself trying to help someone who might be suicidal, your immediate concern should be their safety and the potential causes of these feelings. This is something that should be taken seriously, so it's important that you encourage them to talk to them about how they're feeling, rather than simply trying to cheer them up or dismissing it as a cry for help.

Do not worry that encouraging them to talk openly about suicide will make it more likely to happen - this is not the case. In many cases, simply showing someone that you are there for them, that you want to listen to what they have to say, and they are not alone, can make all the difference in the world.

Do not, however, allow yourself to become their only source of support, as this will only have a negative impact on your own mental health and will not help them as much as professional help would. Try to encourage them to talk to their GP or counsellor about these feelings. Consider discussing strategies together so that they have as many helpful tools as possible if they feel suicidal again in the future, for example by creating a contact lists of organisations, individuals and professionals who will be able to help.

This list can be kept by their phone, and you can encourage them to call someone on the list if they feel suicidal.

In the worst case scenario, if you believe someone you know is at risk of suicide and is refusing to look for help, you can contact social services for help. In severe cases, people can be treated without their consent under the Mental Health Act 1983.

If someone with whom you are in a close personal relationship expresses suicidal feelings, it is likely you will experience strong feelings of frustration, guilt and fear. In this case, you may benefit from support from a family member, friend or support group.

Summing Up

The lower end of the bipolar cycle, depressive episodes can be an extremely trying time. During an episode, it's likely you'll experience an extremely low mood that lasts anywhere from a day or two to several months. It's common to feel useless and utterly drained, with even the simplest daily tasks and interactions seeming beyond impossible.

A number of theories exist which try to explain why we get depressed, but for the most part the causes are similar to those of bipolar disorder: a combination of childhood experiences, stressful events and genetic makeup. Above all, most experts will agree that your perception of the world and of yourself will play a key factor in whether or not you suffer from depression.

Feeling depressed can also have a big impact on how you think. Many people find it difficult to remember things, deter self-effacing or nefative thoughts and concentrate. Your feelings and ability to enjoy life can also be affected, leaving you grumpy, angry and devoid of positive emotions. It is also common to feel lonely and isolated, unable to relate fully to the important people in your life.

Importantly, there's a particularly high risk when you are in a mixed state, depressed or emerging from depression that you may consider attempting suicide. This is something that must be taken seriously by you and those around you. Along with learning the warning signs of suicide, it is absolutely essential that you contact a professional if you believe there is an imminent risk.

At the end of the day, taking care to seek help or support is the best way to keep yourself safe if you are feeling down. As tempting as it may be to hide away from the world when depressed, this is never a good idea. Just keep in mind that there are people around you who care about you, love you, and want to see you get all the help you need.

3

What Causes Bipolar Disorder?

Even after decades of research, we still aren't sure about what exactly causes bipolar. We do, however, have a clearer picture than ever before of what happens in our brains when a mental illness like bipolar disorder develops, thanks to massive advances in the medical fields of neuroscience, brain-imaging and genetics. Recent research shows that changes occur in the chemistry of the brain during depressive and manic episodes. Fluctuations occur in levels of neurotransmitters such as dopamine and serotonin, and of hormones like cortisol, in low and high states, although experts are still trying to determine why exactly this happens.

Analysis is also being carried out of the joints between brain cells (neurons) to determine whether there are any major differences between those of people with and without bipolar disorder. However, whatever the results of these analyses, we will still be unsure whether these differences cause the condition, or the condition causes the differences. What we do know is that illnesses that cause brain injuries, such as strokes and tumours, can lead to bipolar disorder. This suggests that the condition is in some way linked to the interruption of important pathways in the brain.

Could a Faulty Body Clock Be to Blame?

Another current area of interest for experts researching bipolar is that of circadian rhythms. This is the proper term for our body clock, the system in our bodies which controls our eating habits, hormone secretion, body temperature and sleep-wake cycle. Some experts suggest that the mood cycles associated with bipolar, which we have discussed in the previous chapter, could be caused by a body clock which isn't working properly.

The RORB gene - one of the genes controlling the body clock - has been found by researchers at Indiana University to be altered in many children with bipolar disorder. Studies have also found that mood cycles can be improved by strictly regulating the sleep schedule of a patient with bipolar disorder, though experts are yet to figure out why.

Researchers hope to discover the link through research into the RORB gene.

All of this is work that is still in progress, but scientists are hopeful that this research will eventually show the cause of bipolar disorder and, more importantly, how best to treat it. Until then, there are a few things we do know…

'Along with genes, life experience and environmental factors are hugely important.'

Professor Nick Craddock, scientific advisor to MDF: the BiPolar Organisation

Why Your Genes Are So Important

Bipolar is known to run in families, suggesting that there are important genetic factors at play. There is a 1 in 10 chance that children who have one parent with bipolar disorder will

develop the condition themselves, odds which increase to 4 in 10 if both parents have the condition. That said, those conditions sound a lot less worrying if you look at them from the other perspective: Children with one bipolar parent still have a 90% chance of avoiding the condition, while even children with two bipolar parents have a 60% chance of not developing it.

As with many mental illnesses, a large part of the reason you will or will not develop bipolar disorder comes down to genetic predisposition, that is, the likelihood you will develop a condition as a result of your genetic makeup. Strong evidence for this case has come from a number of studies on twins: Where a set of identical twins are brought up in the same environment, there's a 40-70% chance they will both develop the condition. Meanwhile, if the twins are non-identical (meaning they don't share all of the same genes) there's only a 10% chance of both developing bipolar. This strongly suggests that our likelihood of developing the condition is at least partially inherited from our parents.

Despite all of this, we must bare in mind that this doesn't all come down to genetics: there is no such thing as a 'bipolar gene'. It's much more complicated than that. Scientists have discovered that there are a number of genes which can impact the risk of developing bipolar disorder, and that a number of these must come into play in order to have any real effect. There are a great number of people out there who have one or two of the risk variants, who have never developed bipolar because that variant has not had a large enough effect.

The downside of all of this is that the absence of a single 'bipolar gene' makes it impossible to create a simple genetic test which will show how likely you are to develop the condition, although a great deal of work is still being carried out in this area to try and improve diagnosis and treatment as much as possible. Recent research by 24 leading geneticists who collaborate to form the Wellcome Trust Case Control Consortium (WTCC) has discovered new genetic variants for bipolar disorder, among other conditions. This information is very likely to completely change doctors' understanding and treatment of bipolar in our lifetime.

What Are Triggers?

There are a number of factors which are believed to act as 'triggers' in bipolar disorder. Some trigger the development of the condition in people who were previously believed not to suffer it. Others trigger manic or depressive episodes in people who already have the illness. Right now, we're going to talk about the main triggers for bipolar. Later in the book we'll discuss the ways in which you can help yourself by identifying and managing your triggers.

Your Lifestyle

Like any other physical or mental illness, your lifestyle and the world around you play a huge part in bipolar disorder. If you don't have a genetic predisposition towards developing bipolar, your childhood environment - triggers here may include a fighting parents or financial insecurity - and lifestyle choices in later life play a big role in whether you eventually develop the condition.

It's also believed that often stressful circumstances or events are required to trigger the onset of symptoms. These events may include:

- Sexual, emotional or physical abuse

- The death of a loved one, such as a close family member

- A declining relationship

You can't change the family you're born into, or upsetting circumstances such as bereavement. You can, however, change the lifestyle choices you choose to make in order to reduce your likelihood of developing bipolar disorder, regardless of genetic predisposition. As we've discussed, these decisions are especially important in cases where both parents have bipolar. As serious as this sounds, most of these choices are

common-sense, or things we're advised to do by doctors at every standard checkup. You're probably already making some of these healthy lifestyle choices without thinking too much about it:

- Eat a balanced diet with healthy snacks, plenty of fresh vegetables and fruit, and three square meals each day.

- Try to minimise your caffeine intake. If possible, take no more than two caffeinated drinks each day, and keep in mind that many fizzy drinks contain caffeine.

- Avoid illegal drugs such as cocaine, Ecstasy and cannabis. We'll discuss this in more detail in the next point.

- Improve your mood by getting plenty of fresh air and sunlight.

- Maintain a healthy balance between work and real life. Try not to work excessive hours.

- Get plenty of sleep every night. Aim for seven to eight hours.

- Minimise your stress levels.

- Exercise as often as you can. Try to take at least 30 minutes of cardiovascular exercise, five times per week. This can include swimming, brisk walking, cycling or running.

- Try to keep an eye on your alcohol consumption. Find out how many units of alcohol you are allowed each week, and stick to that guideline.

- Don't smoke.

Often, these lifestyle choices are just as important as the genes we inherit, sometimes even more so. Our surroundings and life experiences are crucial when it comes to mental health. Stress, substance abuse and a lack of sleep can all trigger the development of bipolar disorder. Heavy drinking can also contribute to this.

The Dangers of Drugs

You're sure to have been told more times than you can count that illegal drugs are dangerous, especially when taken frequently or in large amounts. This is not surprising, as there is a massive amount of evidence for the fact that drugs such as cocaine, amphetamines, heroin, LSD, Ecstasy and cannabis have a big effect on the chemistry of our brains, and consequently our moods. As we have discussed earlier, these drugs can also be a trigger for developing bipolar.

Importantly, it's not just recreational drugs that need to be carefully monitored. Antidepressants have been found to cause mania and hypomania in almost one third of patients with bipolar disorder. While older antidepressants like amitriptyline are particularly likely to cause mania, it can also result from the upward mood swings caused by more modern SSRI antidepressants like paroxetine and fluoxetine.

This doesn't necessarily mean that antidepressants need to be avoided completely if you have bipolar. It simply means they should be taken with extreme care, and often combined with a drug like lithium to act as a mood-stabiliser. We'll look at this in greater detail in the next chapter.

Substance abuse is very common in those living with bipolar - in fact, it's seen in up to one half of people with the condition, with alcohol the substance most commonly abused. Due to its social acceptability and legality, we tend to forget alcohol is a drug, and consequently it is generally consumed significantly more than all illegal drugs combined. Alcohol has also been found to contribute to the development of depression.

So is it Nature or Nurture?

Experts have argued for some time over whether mental illness is caused by your surroundings and family dynamic (nurture) or your genes (nature). Originally, this was an argument where one side was made up of psychotherapy pioneers (such as Carl Jung and Sigmund Freud) and sociologists, while the other consisted of doctors and psychiatrists. At this stage, the debate is considered irrelevant as most experts in the field believe it to be a combination of both. As we have discussed above, bipolar disorder develops in most cases as a result of a genetic predisposition combined with a trigger such as trauma or substance abuse.

Try thinking of it as you would sunburn: People inherit fair skin from their parents, and it is those with fair skin who are at most risk from sunburn. However, even with fair skin, sunburn is often avoidable by using sunscreen or staying in the shade. Also, even those with darker skin (those without the genetic predisposition for sunburn) can get burnt if they fail to be careful in excessive heat.

Why is Stress a Problem?

At an earlier point in human development (somewhere around 200,000 years ago), we were under constant threats from hostile tribes and terrifying predators. This is why, hundreds of thousands of years later, we have uniquely adapted to survive. We have developed the 'fight, flight or freeze' response to deal with the threats we once dealt with on a daily basis.

Though the vast majority of us are no longer under threats from lions, our brains still deal with perceived threats in a similar way, deciding in mere microseconds whether fight, flight or freeze is the best option. Our body becomes flooded with hormones like adrenaline and noradrenalin to prepare us for an emergency. Our heart starts racing to give our muscles the energy they need to flee or fight, and our breathing speeds up to help oxygenate our blood.

In just a few seconds, even more physical changes are taking place. Our pupils are dilated, our digestive and immune systems have shut down and our palms are sweaty. We are ready for action. The problem is, the threat we're facing is now being pushed in a nightclub our shouted at by our boss, and there's no need to fight or run so the chemicals which have flooded our systems aren't used up and stay in our bodies causing damage.

One of these hormones in particular causes a great amount of damage to our mental and physical health - cortisol. This is the reason chronic stress, especially over extended periods of time, is so detrimental to our health. It can increase our fear, frustration, depression, anger and anxiety, as well as causing indigestion, palpitations, nausea and headaches.

All of this means it's really not surprising that stress is known to be one of the key triggers for those with bipolar disorder. Check our reading list for more information about fight or flight responses.

Can Anything Else Cause Bipolar Disorder?

We have just discussed the main causes of bipolar disorder - both in terms of genetic predispositions and lifestyle factors - but there are still a few lesser-known contributors that we need to know about.

Positive Stress

That negative stressors such as relationship breakdowns, stressful working environments and bereavement can act as triggers for bipolar is both clear and unsurprising. However, it must be noted that some people find even positive life events that happen to be stressful - things like having a baby, getting married and even wedding anniversaries - can act as triggers in some cases.

It is important that you are aware of this fact, and keep in mind that you may need to take extra care of your mental health in the run-up to these events and during these events themselves. That said, many of these events are important parts of a happy, balanced life, so it's important that you allow yourself to enjoy them and do not try to avoid them.

Pregnancy

It has been found that there's a very strong correlation in women living with bipolar between childbirth and experiencing a manic episode. Extra risk comes in the form of a condition referred to as 'postnatal psychosis' (or 'puerperal psychosis') which can lead to the very sudden development of symptoms such as hallucinations, disconnection from reality and general confusion.

None of this means that women with bipolar disorder should never have children. It simply means that the period surrounding the pregnancy should be managed with extra care in these cases, as childbirth can be one of the biggest triggers for mania. Women who have had bipolar mood swings in the past have almost a 50% chance of experiencing a manic episode after childbirth. Knowing this, it's very important that this risk is discussed with your GP, psychiatrist and family in advance.

Known about in advance, women can receive treatment for postnatal psychosis with antipsychotic medication which can stop the symptoms before they become a problem. This is why it is absolutely vital that you (and your loved ones) keep a close eye on your behaviour during this time. We'll talk more about medications in the next chapter.

Why is medication so important?

If you're not convinced that medication will be able to help you, take a look at the following chart, which illustrates the likelihood of having a manic episode with and without medication. Note also how your chance of having another manic episode increases with each past episode. (Information for this table comes from the leaflet Bipolar Disorder (Manic Depression), produced by the Royal College of Psychiatrists.)

Previous Manic Episodes	Likelihood of experiencing an episode in the next year	
	Without Lithium	With Lithium
1-2	1 in 10 (10%)	6-7 in 100 (6-7%)
3-4	1 in 5 (20%)	3 in 25 (12%)
5+	2 in 5 (40%)	13 in 50 (26%)

Seasonal Affective Disorder (SAD)

If you happen to live in the UK or any other Northern European country, there's a high chance you might suffer from seasonal affective disorder (SAD). This is a condition believed to result from the lack of sunlight during winter months, affecting around one million people in the UK alone. Its effects are felt most strongly between the months of September and April, especially in December, January and February.

With this in mind, it's not shocking that these months are also often particularly difficult for those with bipolar disorder or depression. It's believed that the loss of light can cause a biochemical imbalance in the hypothalamus, the part of your brain which regulates appetite, temperature, sex drive, sleep and mood. This is most likely the reason you'll crave comfort foods like crisps, pizza and cake and feel the need to sleep more during these months.

Many experts believe that rather than simply being a separate condition, SAD is a pattern which seasonally affects those already living with bipolar or depression. Up to 38% of people diagnosed with mood disorders are believed to struggle with these seasonal patterns. We will discuss how you can alleviate these symptoms later in the book.

Summing Up

The exact cause of bipolar disorder is not yet known, but it does appear to be related in some way to an imbalance of chemicals in our brains. At present, research is focusing on the roles played by neurotransmitters and hormones, genetic variants, brain cell structures and body clocks. What we do know is that genetic predisposition has a major influence on whether or not we develop bipolar, as there is clear evidence that the condition runs in families. You are more likely to develop bipolar disorder if both of your parents have the condition than if one does, and more likely if one parent has the condition than if neither does.

If you inherit genes which give you a predisposition towards developing the illness, this doesn't necessarily mean you will have bipolar disorder. The condition appears to also require a combination of environmental, lifestyle and traumatic events to develop fully.

4

Which Medications Can Help?

Following your bipolar diagnosis, it's incredibly important that you take any medication you are prescribed. This will be one of your main forms of defence against dangerous moods and episodes of mania (which we will discuss in chapter six), psychosis or depression. Sadly, medication isn't a magic spell that will instantly cure you of bipolar disorder. It can take months, sometimes even years, of working with your doctor and mental health team to perfect your dosage.

Many people also struggle with the fact that this medication will need to be taken for the rest of your life. Doctors can't cure bipolar - like asthma or diabetes, they can only alleviate the symptoms. Fortunately, the medications used to manage bipolar symptoms are currently more effective than ever, and a combination of these along with self-care and talking therapies can improve your symptoms to a significant degree.

One of the most important things to remember when considering bipolar is that, without the proper treatment, this is a condition which can cause significant harm to your mind and body. Aside from symptoms directly caused by the illness, bipolar also often comes

hand-in-hand with drug and alcohol abuse, eating disorders like bulimia or anorexia, or smoking. Those with bipolar also have a much higher rate of coexisting illnesses like high blood pressure and diabetes than the rest of the general population.

Despite all of this, the right treatment combining medication with diet and exercise could help you live a longer, healthier life. It's a good idea to pursue treatment as soon after the development of your symptoms as possible, so that you can work with your mental health team to get the best treatment you can, as soon as you can.

If you find yourself on a medication or dosage you aren't happy with, keep in mind that coming off the medication very suddenly can make you very ill. Nobody will force you to stay on a medication you don't want to be taking, but it is important that you discuss with your doctor first so that you know the safest, most effective way of ending that particular form of treatment.

'I would go so far as saying that, over the years, medication has saved my life.'

Sarah Nayler

How does medication help?

Medications vary based on your symptoms, but the most common types prescribed are a combination of antidepressants, anti-anxiety, andtipsychotic and mood stabilising drugs. Lithium, a mood stabiliser, is the most important medication in the treatment of bipolar, even though it came into use over 60 years ago. This drug is a naturally occurring salt which, despite side effects such as weight gain, often works wonders for people with bipolar disorder.

Sadly, as is the case with most other forms of medication, it's impossible to tell who will experience severe side effects from lithium, and who will find it incredibly helpful. What we do know is that in many cases, those who are relatively stable between manic and depressive episodes and who have a notable family history of bipolar are the most likely to be helped by this drug.

As with many other medications, your doctor will most likely start you on a relatively low dose of lithium and gradually increase the dosage until they have identified your optimum level. Read on for more information about the potential side-effects and reasons for prescribing lithium and other medications, or refer back to the table in Chapter Three for a reminder of why medication is so important.

How mood stabilisers and antipsychotics affect you long term

As with many other parts of life, medications will impact different individuals differently. Your medical professional will be able to explain everything you need to know about the treatment options that are available to you. While the side effects describe may sound serious, keep in mind that not everyone experiences these side effects, and even those who do can experience them in different severities.

Whatever treatment is decided on, you should be given tests at regular intervals to ensure the drug is what works best for you. You can ask your doctor for more information on this, but below we have compiled some of the most common side effects experienced by those on antipsychotics and mood stabilisers.

- Antipsychotics: If you are prescribed the antipsychotic quetiapine, it's advised that you should start on a relatively low dose and slowly increase it. Some have found that they gained weight while taking antipsychotics, and if you have diabetes there is a chance your condition could disimprove.

- Valproate: This medication is rarely offered to women who are pregnant or at risk of becoming pregnant, as it may be harmful to the embryo. Extra care should be taken if you are already on medication for epilepsy, or if you are over the age of 65. Your doctor should also advise you on ways to identify signs of liver or blood problems, as well as what you should do if these symptoms appear.

- Carbamazepine: Carbamazepine should only be taken after consultation with an expert in bipolar. This drug can lead to complications when combined with other medication, including the contraceptive pill, so regular check-ups will be necessary. Dosage of carbamazepine should be increased gradually from a low initial dosage.

- Lamotrigine: As with many other forms of medication, when taking lamotrigine you should start on a low dose and gradually increase it, particularly if you're already taking the drug valproate (see above). This drug must not be taken with the contraceptive pill. If you develop a rash while on lamotrigine, you should seek medical assistance immediately.

- Lithium: If you experience vomiting or diarrhoea while on this drug, be sure to contact your doctor. If possible, avoid taking drugs with an anti-inflammatory effect, such as ibuprofen. If you do not feel the drug is effective, continue taking lithium for at least six months before considering switching to a different medication.

Remember to drink plenty of water, especially after perspiring and if you have pneumonia, a chest infection or are immobile or over the age of 65. When taking lithium, avoid missing doses or stopping the drug suddenly.

Does medication work perfectly every time?

The good news is that we have a number of medications that are proven to be helpful. The bad news is that they're not effective in everybody, and you can't predict who they'll help and who they won't.

So short answer: no. This is how Professor Nick Craddock just how tricky it can be for doctors to try and get your dosage right. Even though we now have a highly sophisticated understanding of how each medication affects our brains, when your doctor initially gives you a prescription they will have no real way of knowing exactly how much it will help.

Although your doctor will be doing their best, this can still be very frustration for the patient, particularly if they find themselves dealing with negative side effects. All you can do is give your GP and psychiatrist as much feedback as you can about how you responded to the medication, and try to be patient.

Even though we have thousands of studies and decades of research under our belts, figuring out which drugs will offer the best treatment for an individual's bipolar symptoms still isn't an exact science. In many cases, finding the right medication comes down to trial and error - though even this is guided by a great amount of literature and trials. Even with lithium, one of the most widely used medications used to treat bipolar disorder, there will be a certain percentage of the population (around 30%) for whom the drug simply won't work.

Importantly, though, even if you are part of the tiny minority for whom lithium will not work, one of the other mood stabilisers available should help instead.

Medication for depression

If you're taking medication for mania, which we will discuss in Chapter Six, and find yourself becoming depressed, you should inform your GP so they can ensure you are being given

the correct dosage. If the depressive symptoms you experience are fairly mild, it's highly unlikely that you'll be offered an medicinal treatment straight away. However, even if this is the case, your doctor should arrange a second appointment within two weeks.

If, by the second meeting, your symptoms have become more severe, you might be prescribed antidepressants. These are drugs which increase your levels of neurotransmitters, natural chemicals which are found in your brain. It is these chemicals that regulate or control a number of your bodily functions, including your mood. Experts believe that depression is caused by a lack of the neurotransmitters serotonin and noradrenalin.

Your antidepressants will take somewhere between 2 and 8 weeks to start working, so you should continue to take them even if they don't appear to be having an effect initially. In some cases, individuals are able to come off their antidepressants as soon as their depressive episode has ended, but in others you will have to stay on the medication for a number of months. It all depends on how you have reacted to antidepressants in the past.

If avoidable, antidepressants should not be taken for too long after the depression has been resolved, otherwise there's a risk of triggering a hypomanic or manic episode. This mustn't be done suddenly, though: dosage should be gradually reduced over a number of weeks.

The following are some of the most commonly used antidepressants at present.

Tricyclic Antidepressants (TCSs)

- Allegron (nortriptyline)
- Anafranil (clomipramine)
- Prothiaden (dothiepin)
- Sinepin (doxepin)
- Surmontil (trimipramine)

- Lomont (lofepramine)
- Imipramine
- Anafranil SR (clomipramine)
- Amitriptyline

It is relatively unusual for tricyclic antidepressants to be prescribed to those with bipolar disorder, as they come with a high risk of causing mania. TCAs are also prone to causing drowsiness, especially in the cases of dothiepin and amitriptyline (though this can be beneficial to those who are restless or anxious). Tricyclic antidepressants like lofepramine and imipramine have less of a sedative effect than others.

TCAs can bring with them a variety of other side effects which can include difficulty in urinating, dry mouth, weight gain, blurred vision and constipation. It is strongly advised that those who suffer from heart disease should not be prescribed tricyclic antidepressants.

Drugs such as venlafaxine work in a similar way to TCAs, but without producing these side effects. They do, however, carry a higher risk of causing manic episodes.

Selective Seretonin Reuptake Inhibitors (SSRIs)

These include:

- Cipralex (escitalopram)
- Prozac (fluoxetine)
- Lustral (sertraline)
- Seroxat (paroxetine)
- Cipramil (citalopram)
- Faverin (fluvoxamine)

Fewer negative side effects are generally experienced by those using SSRIs than by those prescribed the older MAOIs (Monoamine oxidase inhibitors) and tricyclics. For this reason, they're the antidepressant most commonly used by people with bipolar disorder. SSRIs are also less likely than many antidepressants to cause hypomania or mania in those with bipolar.

Of the SSRIs listed above, fluoxetine is generally used the least often as it stays in the body for a long time after treatment is ended. This has the potential to cause issues if a manic episode means treatment needs to be stopped quickly.

As they have far fewer sedative effects than older types of antidepressant, SSRIs are more suitable for people who feel their depression slows them down, and especially those with heart problems. That said, people taking SSRIs may still have to deal with a few negative side effects including vomiting, constipation, diarrhoea and nausea. Other side effects can include dizziness, insomnia, agitation and headaches.

While all antidepressants have been found to be linked with sexual difficulties like impotence, this issue seems to occur most frequently with SSRIs.

Monoamine oxidase inhibitors (MAOIs)

- Isocarboxazid
- Nardil (phenelzine)
- Tranylcypromine
- Manerix (moclobemide)

As a general rule, monoamine oxidase inhibitors are prescribed far less often than other types of antidepressant as they require strict restrictions to the person's diet, owing to how they react to certain food types. They also carry the risk of causing severe reactions when combined with other medications, even including over the counter cold and flu medicines.

A newer type of MAOI, moclobemide is more likely to be prescribed than other MAOIs. This drug appears to cause fewer adverse effects than other similar medications, but it's still advised that those taking this medication exercise great caution around certain medicines and foods.

Summing Up

If you have bipolar, it's vital that you take the medication necessary to control your mood and avoid mania, psychosis or depression. As with conditions like diabetes or asthma, however, bipolar is a condition which will be with you for your whole life and can only be managed, not cured. On the upside, as well as improving your quality of life, effective treatment could actually lengthen your life expectancy.

Effective treatment will generally consist of a combination of medications like mood stabilisers, anti-anxiety drugs, antipsychotics and antidepressants. A naturally occurring salt called lithium is the most effective and thus most commonly prescribed bipolar medication, helping to stabilise the moods of about 70% of those who take it. As with other drugs, though, it is not effective for everyone and may cause some side effects.

Even after decades of research, we have no way of working out who will and won't find different medications helpful, so even healthcare professionals will rely on a process of trial and error when finding the right drug and dosage for you. Although all medications take a while to begin working, it's important that you be patient and continue taking them for as long as is necessary. If you really must stop taking a certain medication, do so gradually and with consent and advice from your psychiatrist.

5

Getting a Diagnosis

t is incredibly important that those with bipolar receive a professional diagnosis as early in the development of the condition as possible, as this will give the best chance of successful treatment and positive long-term outcomes. It's believed that it is generally significantly easier to successfully treat someone who has had less than three episodes. Beyond this point, the condition tends to get more difficult to treat with each episode.

Unfortunately, for most people with bipolar, diagnoses are not made before the third episode. This is something we'll explore in greater detail later in the book.

As with many other mental health condition, it can take years to receive a proper diagnosis, and many mental health professionals will not recognise you as having bipolar disorder without at least one severe manic episode. As we discussed in Chapter One, this means it's also very unlikely that your GP will be willing or able to diagnose you with bipolar disorder. They will either give you a misdiagnosis, or will refer you to a psychiatrist who will be able to give you a more accurate diagnosis. This can be deeply frustrating, but the importance of this diagnosis makes it worth the wait, and you can use this waiting time to familiarise yourself with the condition, potential treatments, services provided by mental health professionals and things that you can do yourself to alleviate your symptoms.

Will You Have to Stay in Hospital?

As a general rule, you should be able to receive the vast majority of your treatment without having to stay in a hospital. However, if you are receiving treatment under the Mental Health Act or your symptoms are particularly severe you may be admitted to hospital for a time.

Some patients are also offered treatment in day hospitals. In this case, they may spend most of the day in the hospital in order to receive treatment but will go back to their own homes in the evening.

If doctors begin to feel you may pose a risk to yourself or others, or you are experiencing acute mental distress and refuse treatment, there is a chance you could be 'sectioned'. This word means that you are forcibly admitted to hospital to receive the necessary treatment for your condition. It's important to keep in mind that 'sectioning' is reserved for when doctors believe it is absolutely necessary to do so. The vast majority of patients only receive treatment with their express consent, with sectioning happening only in very extreme circumstances.

'I'd never heard the word before, but for the first time, at the age of 37, I had a diagnosis that explains the massive highs and miserable lows I've lived with all my life.'

Stephen Fry

How Does a Psychiatrist Know if it's Mania?

When you meet with a psychiatrist for assessment, they will compare the symptoms you experienced with those listed in the DSM IV (or with those listed in the International Classification of Diseases, version 10 (ICD10)). This list will include a selection of factors which must be experienced before your condition is classified as mania. Firstly, your mood will need to be uninhibited, irritable or elevated, and distinct from your usual mood when stable.

In order for the second major criterion to be met, at least three of these symptoms must be present to a considerable degree:

- Heightened sense of self-importance
- Increased talkativeness

- Highly distractible
- Increased amounts of pleasurable (yet poorly considered) activities, such as excessive spending or extramarital affairs
- Higher levels of activity in pursuit of goals
- Erratic thoughts and ideas
- Reduced need for sleep

The third criterion states that in order for the patient to be diagnosed with mania, their symptoms must affect their relationships or performance at work. This factor is included in order to distinguish between mania, which features very severe symptoms, and hypomania, whose symptoms are slightly milder.

Some questions you may be asked in order to determine this are as follows:

- Do you experience periods of high work rate and energy?
- Do you ever feel as though you are the best at everything you do?
- Do you feel that your thoughts are hyperactive?
- Do you believe you have magical powers, or hear voices that aren't there?
- Do you tend to sleep too little?
- Have you ever experienced difficulties during these periods as a result of overspending or overborrowing?
- How indignant or happy do you tend to get, and how long do these moods last?

What happens during a manic episode?

(A)n extreme sense of wellbeing, energy and optimism. It can be so intense that it affects your thinking and judgement. You may believe strange things about yourself, make bad decisions, and behave in embarrassing, harmful and – occasionally – dangerous ways.

This is how the mania is described on the Roual College of Psychiatrists' website (www.rcpsych.ac.uk). As with every other part of bipolar, the symptoms you will experience during a manic episode - along with their length and severity - will vary from person to person. However, there are a few experiences that are commonly described by people with bipolar disorder.

We have already the symptoms of mania in Chapter One, but will repeat them here as a reminder:

- Strong feelings of excitement and happiness
- Feeling extremely important
- Constant movement from one idea to the next
- Unwillingness or inability to sleep
- Unrealistic, grandiose plans
- Odd behaviour
- Making decisions recklessly
- Hyper-criticality and overfamiliarity with others
- Generally reduced inhibitions
- Impulsive spending
- Talking unusually quickly
- Compulsion to move around
- Increased sex drive
- Unlimited energy
- Suddenly filled with exciting new ideas
- Irritation with anyone who doesn't share your optimism

As with depression (see Chapter Two), mania is about more than just a changed mood. Its symptoms entail altered thinking, behaviour, bodily sensations and emotions. These episodes can last for anywhere between two weeks and five months when left untreated.

An important thing to note is that if you're experiencing your first manic episode, you might not even notice it happening. Especially at the start of the episode, when the symptoms have not yet snowballed out of control, you'll simply feel confident, energized and happy. For this reason, you're likely to have no strong desire to contact your GP - why would you?

Those around you, however, are more likely to notice that your behaviour is more than just the result of a good mood. If they point this out to you, you may well feel offended, but it's very important that you pay attention and get help if it seems necessary.

How do they know if it's depression?

There are several criteria outlined in the DSM-IV in order to distinguish major depression from mild or moderate depression. In order to be diagnosed with this condition, patients need to have experienced depression for two or more weeks, exhibiting at least five of the following symptoms:

- Low mood lasting for the majority of the day, nearly every day
- Changes in appetite and weight
- Reduced physical activity
- Excessive feelings of remorse and worthlessness
- Suicidal ideation
- Difficulty concentrating
- Reduced energy and fatigue
- Disrupted sleep
- Reduced enjoyment or interest in most activities, nearly every day

Of the five symptoms a patient must experience, two must be the reduced interest in activities and low mood. The psychiatrist will often ask follow-up questions in order to determine the patient's mental health history, lifestyle and anxiety levels.

How do they know if it's psychosis?

Psychosis will not necessarily affect everyone with bipolar, but it is something that can happen during severe manic episodes. This condition is characterised by unusual changes in basic cognitive, judgemental, affective and perceptual processes, or how you think about, judge, feel and perceive things. Those suffering from psychosis may experience hallucinations, disorganised behaviour and speech, and delusions. During the assessment, the psychiatrist will ask questions to determine whether you have exhibited any of these symptoms. If they find that you have, you will be prescribed an antipsychotic medication to eliminate or reduce symptoms. We'll discuss these symptoms in more detail later in the book.

What is schizoaffective disorder?

According to the DSM-IV, schizoaffective disorder is the 'presence of psychotic symptoms in the absence of mood changes for at least two weeks in a person who has a mood disorder.' It is generally diagnosed when a patient doesn't have the typical symptoms for a mood disorder or schizophrenia, instead exhibiting a combination of symptoms from both types of disorder.

Schizoaffective disorder is often misdiagnosed as bipolar disorder. This is because, as a very complex illness, it is often very hard to diagnose correctly. If you feel this is an accurate description of your own symptoms, you should ask your psychiatrist or another mental health professional to arrange an assessment.

Case study

Chris, a former teacher and now writer and broadcaster, was originally diagnosed with unipolar depression – a very common misdiagnosis, because most people with bipolar disorder experience several depressive episodes before one of mania. He also explains how finally getting a correct diagnosis was a massive relief, because it helped him to understand the swings between huge success and subsequent failure which had dominated his life.

'I was originally diagnosed with unipolar depression in 1998. After a year off work, I was pensioned off from my job as deputy head of a catholic school in Southend. I was prescribed Prozac, but I suffered badly on it and became very ill. That ended up destroying my first marriage.

'About five years after the misdiagnosis, which was from a private hospital, I went to see an NHS consultant. He took my history and said he didn't think I had unipolar depression at all, and that I had been a manic depressive my whole life.

'That was a great relief to me, because it explained the pattern of my life, which had been enormous successes followed by enormous failures. It was as if I had an unerring capacity both to achieve and to press the self-destruct button, which I think is fairly typical of manic depressives.

'Once I got the new diagnosis, through a combination of new medication and psychotherapy, I became very much better. So the last five years have been an increasingly improving picture. We've now hit on a drugs regime – sodium valproate and Lamotrigine, both mood stabilisers, plus Duloxetine, an antidepressant – that keeps me stable, stops me being suicidal or dangerously manic.'

What questions should I ask?

If you're not sure what questions you should ask your psychiatrist following diagnosis, these are a few helpful questions that should get you the information you need (as described in the NICE Clinical Guidelines on Bipolar Disorder). For more on the type of information you should receive as a patient, refer back to Chapter One's section on your rights as a patient.

- What leads you to believe I have bipolar disorder?
- Are all of the symptoms I've experienced caused by bipolar?
- What could this mean for my physical health?
- Are there any early warning signs for manic or depressive episodes that I should be aware of?
- How might this condition affect my day-to-day life?
- What do you think is likely to have caused my bipolar disorder?

What support can you expect from healthcare professionals?

Your healthcare professional should give you general advice about coping with your symptoms, such as how to spot the early warning signs of an episode and how to sleep well and have a regular lifestyle. They should also tell you about self-help groups and support groups.

These are the NICE guidelines on what you should be able to expect from your healthcare professionals. As we've already discussed, it's incredibly important that you and your loved ones are as informed as possible about what you should expect following your diagnosis. Bipolar disorder is an illness and as with any other illness, helpful information is your most important tool in managing symptoms.

Knowledge is also your shield against misinformation. Receiving a diagnosis, especially one of a lifelong condition such as bipolar, can be stressful enough without frightening rumours and misinformation.

Some people react with grief or anger on receiving a diagnosis of a mental illness, because they worry about how the social stigma around mental health conditions will affect the way they are treated. It falls on healthcare professionals to relieve some of this anger and sadness by providing patients with all of the help and information they require.

The information you are provided by your healthcare professionals should allow you to make an informed decision about the type of care that's right for you. However, if you're experiencing very severe symptoms, you may not be in a position to express your needs or make these important decisions. It's often a good idea to compose a set of written directions or 'advanced directives' when you are able, which will explain the assistance and treatment you would like to receive in this situation. Another role of a healthcare professional is to help you draw up these instructions.

Finally, it is recommended that if you experience severe depression or manic episodes, your mental health team should arrange to meet you for a second time within a week of your initial assessment. They should continue meeting with you on a regular basis from this point onwards, perhaps every 2-4 weeks for the first few months and then slightly less frequently if the treatment appears to be working.

Who will treat you?

In most cases, those with bipolar will get the majority of their treatment from a CMHT (community mental health team) consisting of a CPN (community psychiatric nurse), OT (occupational therapist), pharmacist, clinical psychologist, social worker and psychiatrist. Your GP will also play an important role in the treatment you receive, so you should be sure you make an appointment with your psychiatrist if you move to a different GP practice.

Additional appointments should be offered to you if you are believed to pose a risk to yourself or those around you, if you have alcohol or drug problems, if your treatment doesn't appear to be working or if your symptoms become significantly worse.

You should be given appointments on a regular basis, preferably receiving treatment from the same healthcare professionals each time. In the event you receive treatment from numerous healthcare professionals, there should be clear information available about the role each of them plays in your treatment.

A spectrum disorder

We all have experience of mood varying and sometimes we're much more down than at others. And there are lots of people in the general population who might have severe ups and downs that don't cause a problem, so it would be silly to see that as an illness. It's only when it becomes very severe and disabling that we would talk about it being an illness.

This is how Professor Craddock explains a merge between bipolar disorder and 'normality.' It has been estimated that almost 70% of patients with bipolar disorder initially receive the wrong diagnosis, with an average delay of eight years before the correct diagnosis is made (see 'Why is bipolar misdiagnosed?' in Chapter One). In order to understand why this misdiagnosis is so common, it can be useful to keep in mind that bipolar disorder is a 'spectrum disorder.'

The symptoms of those with the condition can range to a very mild one percent to a very severe 100%. Those at the lower end of the spectrum may only swing between hypomania and mild depression, and in many cases have no need for treatment at all. Some with this condition have found that hypomania can even be a real asset, thriving in creative industries as a result of their bursts of imagination and energy.

Hopefully, this information will make it clear to the reader just why bipolar disorder can be so difficult to diagnose, even for highly experienced psychiatrists. These professionals rely on what their patients tell them in order to make a diagnosis, and there is little they can do if their patient has only experienced depression or has experienced mild highs but hasn't deemed them noteworthy enough to tell a medical professional.

Hard work is going into research that hopes to improve the methods of treatment and diagnosis. But until this research is complete, it is your own responsibility to talk to your psychiatrist or GP if you think you may have been misdiagnosed.

Summing Up

It's incredibly important that bipolar is diagnosed as early as it can be, as treatment will be more effective if it begins early in the condition's development. However, as most individuals will experience a few depressive episodes before mania, it's very often misdiagnosed as major depression initially.

Often, it's only when the patient experiences a severe manic episode involving police intervention or hospitalisation that an accurate diagnosis is made. This diagnosis will involve an assessment carried out by a psychiatrist, who will ask questions about mania, psychosis, anxiety and depression as well as about your lifestyle and family medical history.

Once you have received your diagnosis, you'll have a right to expect a high standard of treatment from a team of mental health professionals. You and your family will receive the best support and help if you have as much information about bipolar and its treatment as possible, allowing an understanding of your preferred methods of treatment and support.

6

Mania (the highs)

Everyone goes through periods where they feel more optimistic, energetic, exciteable and happy than usual. With bipolar, however, this is more than just a good mood: these are feelings which can escalate until you're talking too quickly for people around you to understand, or you're convinced you can do anything from writing a bestseller to learning fluent Latin over the space of a weekend, or you feel as though you'll never need to sleep again. Some people describe the escalation of a manic episode as a snowball effect: it begins slowly, but gathers speed and is soon growing larger and faster uncontrollably.

Bouts of lifted mood and energy which are similar but milder are known as 'hypomania.' This is an incredibly common condition, with researchers believing that large sections of the population - especially those involved in creative industries such as the media, performing arts and advertising - will experience this at one time or another. While only causing minor issues in itself, hypomania can easily escalate into full mania if left unchecked, which is a far more severe and troublesome condition.

Some people with bipolar disorder also experience psychosis, where mania becomes extreme to the point where they entirely lose touch with reality. However, this condition does not affect all people with bipolar.

How do manic symptoms develop?

Experts believe that manic symptoms occur as a result of a vicious cycle including thoughts, bodily changes, behaviour and mood. For example, an individual may experience a positive, energized mood which leads them to think that they are in the perfect position to begin working on as many projects as possible. Their behaviour alters as they begin to take on more challenges and increase their productivity, sometimes working all the way through the night. This extra activity will lead to bodily changes like exhaustion, from which they will eventually emerge and experience their positive mood once again.

> 'Seven years ago I had an attack of pathological enthusiasm. I believed I could stop cars and paralyse their forces by merely standing in the middle of the highway with my arms outspread.'
>
> Robert Lowell, Pulitzer Prize-winning poet

It is believed that the four elements of this cycle will get more severe over time, until the individual begins experiencing hypomania or mania. Although the cycle and resulting condition are very serious, people can learn to alter the cycle through CBT (cognitive behavioural therapy).

What is CBT?

Believed by the Department of Health to be the most effective form of psychological treatment available, cognitive behavioural therapy (CBT) is receiving a large amount of attention at the moment. In fact, thousands of CBT therapists are currently being trained as part of the Improving Access to Therapies (IAPT) programme. While some experts worry that other practices are being neglected as a result of this focus, a great amount of research shows that CBT can treat a large variety of conditions and thus is worthy of this focus.

Along with bipolar disorder, CBT has been found to be effective in treating depression, phobias, bulimia, post-traumatic stress disorder, psychosis, obsessive-compulsive disorder, stress, panic and anxiety. Its goal is to alter the ways in which you think (cognitive) and act (behaviour) to help you feel better. Unlike some of the other approaches available, CBT's primary focus is on the difficulties and problems you face in the current day. The aim is to improve your present state of mind.

The key aspect of cognitive behavioural therapy is that it helps you change your thought processes, with a focus on those which are seen as destructive or negative. CBT therapists would argue that the way in which you think about things can have a massive impact on the way you feel, on your mood and emotions. This then goes on to affect your behaviour.

Through CBT, you can break down problems which seem overwhelming into small, manageable parts. These parts can be summarised as:

- Situation (e.g. your boss yelled at you at work)
- Your thoughts (e.g. 'he always picks on me, he must hate me')
- Your feelings (e.g. unhappy, frustrated, angry, low)
- Your behaviour (e.g. avoiding work the next day by pretending to have the flu)

Your therapist will then be able to replace these unhelpful responses with more practical thoughts and actions. For example, they may encourage you to think about why your boss is shouting at you: is it more likely that they hate you, or that they're simply having a bad day? This greater understanding may actually lead to a stronger relationship with your boss, removing the need to call in sick the next day.

How mania affects behaviour

I think the ups are most destructive for people with bipolar… People can get into an awful lot of trouble in a very limited period of time. Sexual indiscretions, spending a lot of money, making a fool of themselves in public. It might only last a few days, but living it down can be a long-term process.

This is how Dr Cosmo Hallstrom, fellow of the Royal College of Psychiatrists, explains the issues that come with mania. One of the main problems associated with manic episodes is the impact they have on your decision-making and general behaviour. It is a condition which can become incredibly destructive to your relationships with friends, loved ones and work colleagues.

Mania can make it difficult to understand the affect your actions and words have on those around you, causing confusion and sometimes frustration about why others aren't sharing in your joke. Mania may also cause you to experience grandiose delusions that you can solve every problem your friends and family have, or even every problem on earth.

It can even cause you to become incredibly over-critical or over-friendly, and exhibit other such inappropriate behaviours. In some cases, this will simply cause confusion in the other people involved. However, it also has the potential to cause real offence and tension.

Mania and debt

One big issue faced by those in the midst of a manic episode is that of over-spending. Reports have found that those who have experienced mental distress - such as the distress associated with bipolar - are up to three times more likely to find themselves in debt than the rest of the general population. In fact, these statistics rose to four times for people with bipolar.

It becomes clear why people with bipolar disorder struggle with these issues when we look at the symptoms associated with a manic episode. A manic episode may cause you to make strange, spur of the moment decisions like buying rounds for a bar full of strangers, buying designer clothes, property or a new car, or placing a large bet. It could even cause you to make ill-advised, grandiose plans like starting a business or investing in suspicious get-rich-quick schemes.

All of this suggests that having access to all of your savings and credit is, perhaps, not the best idea during a manic episode. If you think this could be an issue for you, you could try requesting a cap to be placed on your spending, or cutting up your cards so you cannot use them. Try to listen to the advice of professionals - both medical and financial - and of those who care about you. If you find yourself in debt, don't hesitate to look for help from organisation such as x, y and z.

Mania and sex

As explained by Dr. Hallstrom, one of the troublesome aspects of mania is the increased sex drive and reduced inhibitions. Just as depression can decrease your confidence, libido and energy, mania can increase them. This can often lead people to go to greater lengths to attain sexual conquests, or simply to misread someone's signals as meaning more than they really do.

At times, this means people with bipolar disorders can find themselves in risky situations such as engaging in unprotected sex or being identified as a target for sexual violence. It is common for people experiencing mania or hypomania to be reluctant to listen to the concerns of those around them, especially when it comes to sensitive topics such as this one, but it's important that you pay attention to the advice of those you trust.

If you believe you have engaged in unprotected sex and are at risk of having contracted an STI, free and confidential advice can be acquired through your GP or local GUM (genito-urinary medicine) clinic. Information on those can be found through the NHS Choices website - www.nhs.uk.

Case study

Robert Westhead, 36, works for Shift, a campaign against stigmatising mental illness. He describes the extreme episodes of mania he experienced as a teenager, before getting a diagnosis and receiving treatment – and how those episodes spilled over into psychosis

'While travelling abroad during a year off I became seriously ill. I'd been travelling in India and at one point my mood swings started becoming regular and increasingly severe – not ordinary mood swings.

'I would get very down for a week or 10 days, then would suddenly be the life and soul of the party. I remember being in Kashmir and suddenly feeling unaccountably happy, sociable, witty and full of energy.

'When I got home and my parents met me off the plane, I was talking ten to the dozen and telling them I didn't need to sleep – when you're high you become more and more ill and can literally go without sleep. My parents didn't know what to think.

'The illness got more and more extreme. My highs were getting worse and I was losing all sense of reality. I was constantly talking and my speech became so fast I stopped making sense. I was spouting poetry and behaving very oddly, like dashing back to my old school and taking over lessons.

'I also had psychotic delusions, especially religious ones – I thought I was on some kind of mission from God and remember seeing God's face in the smallest things, like a light switch or God staring out at me from cracks in the pavement.'

What is psychosis?

(Psychotic symptoms) tend to be grandiose beliefs about yourself – that you are on an important mission or that you have special powers and abilities.

This is how the Royal College of Psychiatrists describes psychotic symptoms on their website. At times, a severe manic episode may lead to a loss of contact with reality, also known as psychosis. These symptoms can also develop during a period of depression, leading to beliefs that you are worse than everyone else, that you don't exist or that you are uniquely guilty. Some individuals even experience hallucinations during psychosis, smelling, seeing, feeling or hearing things that aren't really there.

Interestingly, psychotic symptoms often seem to incorporate some sort of spiritual or religious experience. Many people with bipolar come to believe they have been sent by a deity to bring an end to poverty or begin world peace. Others believe they have been given supernatural powers, like telepathy. In many cases, those with bipolar disorder will struggle with paranoia, often causing them to become hypersensitive to anything which could be perceived as a slight or an insult.

Always keep in mind that not everyone who has bipolar will have to deal with psychosis. If you do, however, begin to experience any of the symptoms described above, you can inform your community mental health team or GP who will be able to prescribe the right medication to relieve these symptoms.

Treatments for episodes of mania or hypomania

Your psychiatrist will be following a set of guidelines (such as the NICE Guidelines for Carers) when working out which medications should be prescribed to treat your hypomania or mania. Here are a few of the medications you may hear about:

- Quetiapine, risperidone or olanzapine (antipsychotics): These drugs are often prescribed if your behaviour is disturbed or if the symptoms you exhibit are severe.

- Valproate: This medication is sometimes offered if it has helped with your symptoms in the past, but is rarely prescribed to pregnant women as it could harm the unborn child.

- Valium or Xanax (benzodiazepines): This medication may be offered along with an antipsychotic to help improve your sleep and calm you down.

- Lithium: This drug is usually prescribed if your symptoms are relatively mild.

Is there an upside to mania?

The illness provides experiences and a view of the world that those who have not been there can never appreciate.

This is how Jeremy Thomas explains how his experience with bipolar disorder has enriched his life in the book You Don't Have to be Famous to Have Manic Depression. While it is important to avoid implying that mania (and by extension bipolar) is not a serious condition, it can be nice to finish on a reminder that it's not all doom and gloom. In a survey run by the Doctors Support Network, a group which provides support for doctors dealing with mental illnesses, 95% of those surveyed were able to find something positive about their condition.

For example, some stated that they were able to have a greater sense of maturity and self-awareness, or more empathy for their patients.

Of course, we've already discussed another positive earlier in the text: hypomania, a milder form of mania, is often seen in creatives such as artists, comedians and writers, who may not have managed to produce their work without the erratic energy that came with the condition.

Summing Up

It's simply part of the human condition that people will go through periods where they feel more energetic, positive and happy than usual. However, for those with bipolar, these feelings can easily turn into a manic or hypomanic episode of exceptional confidence, chattiness, euphoria, distractibility and reduced sleep which can last for days or weeks.

For some - especially those with Bipolar II - their condition will only consist of hypomania, stability and depression. However, for those with Bipolar I, this hypomania can evolve into full-blown mania without treatment, resulting in excitability, refusal to sleep and irritability. In many cases, the condition can even cause an increased sex drive and impulsive

decision-making, which can result in real problems.

Often, people who are experiencing their first manic or hypomanic episode won't even notice anything is wrong. Why would you consider improved confidence, energy and creativity to be a bad thing? The people around you, however, are more likely to notice strange behaviour. You may not feel like taking their advice if it offends or annoys you, but the people who love you are only trying to keep you safe.

It's especially important to take advice from professionals and loved ones when it comes to overspending and risky sexual behaviour, two of the most common problems for people experiencing mania. If you're worried about finding yourself in debt as a result of overspending, there are plenty of organisations out there who can help. Meanwhile, if you've engaged in unprotected sex, it's a good idea to meet with your GP to discuss getting checked for sexually transmitted infections (STIs).

Some people with bipolar disorder also go through periods of manic and depressive symptoms at the same time, known as mixed states. Others experience psychosis, which may cause them to hallucinate or have delusional thoughts. If you believe you are experiencing either of these conditions, try to talk to a mental health professional or GP as soon as you can.

7

Talking Therapies

There are three main areas when it comes to treating bipolar. Medication, which we discussed in Chapter Four, is the primary treatment. No matter what other treatment you undergo, it is vital that you remember to take your medication every day in order to manage your symptoms effectively. Self-care, which we will discuss later, is also an important step in taking control over your condition.

The third part of your treatment for bipolar disorder is the talking therapies, which we will discuss in this chapter. As the name would suggest, talking therapies involve you talking to a professional about any issues you have, either individually or as part of a group. A great amount of research has found that a combination of talking therapies and medication is significantly more effective than medication on its own. This means it's important for you to have a good understanding of the different approaches and their effects, as well as how long they take to be effective and whether you need to access them through the NHS or through private healthcare.

How do talking therapies help?

We can all benefit from sitting down every now and then to talk to someone who will listen without judging or being overly critical. This is a service offered by all good therapists and counsellors, no matter what types of talking therapy they are trained in. Extensive research has been carried out into the ways in which counselling helps us, and it's been found that the most important contributor to the effectiveness of this treatment is the relationship between client and counsellors. This matters more than the therapist's experience, skills or even what techniques they practice.

This is no less the case if you are receiving treatment for bipolar. However, it's also important that your therapist offers help which will enable you to manage your mood swings, such as knowing how to avoid full-blown episodes and how to identify warning signs as early in the cycle as possible. So whatever type of talking therapy you settle on, try to make sure it's one which has been proven to help clients with bipolar.

'A man is but the product of his thoughts. What he thinks, he becomes.'

Mahatma Gandhi

Interestingly, experts once believed that bipolar was an illness with purely biological causes, and one which could therefore only be treated with medication. This is no longer the belief, however, as a great amount of research has shown that talking therapies are incredibly important in managing bipolar symptoms.

One such study, carried out by the University of Colorado, has found that introducing intensive psychotherapy to the treatment of a patient with bipolar disorder helped the patient recover from depressive episodes far more quickly. Patients receiving therapy were also 1.5 times more likely to be considered 'clinically well' during any particular month than those without therapy.

In this chapter, we'll look at some of the most common talking therapies used in the treatment of patients with bipolar.

Cognitive Behavioural Therapy

As we discussed in Chapter 4, the key aspect of cognitive behavioural therapy is that it helps you change your thought processes, with a focus on those which are seen as destructive or negative. CBT therapists would argue that the way in which you think about things can have a massive impact on the way you feel, on your mood and emotions. This then goes on to affect your behaviour.

What happens in CBT sessions?

As a general rule, you and your CBT therapist will meet between 5 and 20 times, on a weekly or fortnightly basis. Sessions usually last between 30 and 60 minutes. In the first couple of sessions, the therapist will explain exactly what this sort of treatment will entail, and make sure you are comfortable continuing. They'll also ask questions to find out more about your background and everyday life. While the focus of this therapy will be on the here and now, it can be helpful to talk about the past in order to work out how it might be affecting you today.

From there, treatment will involve the following factors:

- Deciding what issues you want help with in the short, medium and long term. You and your therapist will generally also start each session by discussing what you want to talk about that day.

- Looking at your thought patterns, emotions and actions. Together, you can decide which responses were helpful or unhelpful, realistic or unrealistic. You can then figure out how these behaviours affect you and those around you.

- Doing your homework. Some therapists give homework, usually asking you to practice methods you have discussed in your everyday life.

- Working out how to alter unrealistic thought processes and actions.

- Breaking problems down into their separate parts. To help with this, you might be asked to begin keeping a diary so that you can keep a record of your thought patterns, feelings and actions.

How CBT can help regulate your moods

For each individual you work out their cycle of mood escalation and how that impacts on their behaviour and other people. That's not just about identifying individual symptoms, but the whole process of how their mood develops, the relationship between their thoughts, feelings, behaviour and environment that drives their mood into problematic areas.

This is how Warren Mansell, senior psychology lecturer in the University of Manchester, works with his bipolar clients. One of the main reasons people with bipolar tend to find cognitive behavioural therapy so useful is that it can be very effective in identifying when, why and how their mood swings occur.

Often, those with bipolar disorder will describe their feelings as something to do with themselves, rather than a result of their environment. However, emotions are generally influenced by a combination of external factors - such as the nature of someone's work - and internal ones like self-critical or otherwise negative thoughts. It is your CBT therapist's job to help you understand how these factors work together to impact your mood.

A good cognitive behavioural therapist will also aid you in detecting warning signs for your mood swings. For example, for an episode of depression, warning signs might include:

- Negative thoughts
- Reduced energy levels
- A lack of motivation and reduced interest in sociable activities
- Reduced sex drive and appetite
- Interrupted/insufficient sleep
- Feelings of anxiety

Meanwhile, for a manic episode, warning signs might include:

- Racing thoughts
- Increased sense of self-worth
- Feelings of restlessness, overexcitement and sociability
- Overspending
- New focus on goal-oriented activities like redecorating your house or planning an event
- Reduced need for sleep
- Irritability

Once your warning signs have been identified, it becomes easier to prevent your mood swings from evolving into full-blown depression or mania. However, it's also important to remember that a certain amount of variation in your mood is entirely normal and healthy. CBT teaches that a mood doesn't need to be a problem, that it's the way in which we think about the mood that turns it into a problem. Moods themselves only become a problem when they lead to strange or harmful behaviours. CBT aims to help people with bipolar disorder identify their cycles of thought and behaviour around certain moods, and learn how to change their responses to something healthier.

Keep in mind that everyone's moods change from time to time. It is only when they begin to interfere with your life or the lives of those around you that you should begin to worry.

Case study

Jonathan Naess worked as a lawyer in the City before leaving to set up Stand to Reason, a charity that tackles the stigma associated with mental illness. He describes how CBT has helped him manage his bipolar disorder.

'When I'm depressed, I find it really hard to get out of bed and find it difficult to do anything constructive. So a lot of my initial work with a CBT therapist was on simple, practical stuff, just to get me moving again and slowly build up some momentum. I'm a real perfectionist and give myself a very hard time if I'm not doing a million things every day, so the therapist taught me to lower my expectations and allow myself to do just two or three things in a day.

'I can also get very isolated when I'm depressed – I could easily not leave the house for a week. So another key thing we worked on was making sure I saw people, actually putting that in my diary so I saw at least one person a day. I was really struggling at the time, so breaking it down into simple steps, doing small constructive things, did help lift me out of my depression.

'Another thing we worked on was having at least one thing every week to look forward to. I couldn't even think about doing vigorous exercise, but I was just about up to a round of golf. That gave me something enjoyable to focus on too.

'Once we had worked on that behavioural stuff, we worked on my thinking patterns. I began to see that the language I used about myself was very negative. So I learned that being kind to myself was very important, instead of judging myself so harshly, because, of course, that brings you down. It's a vicious circle you need to interrupt.

'As well as the CBT work, I also found the self-help groups run by MDF – the BiPolar Organisation really useful. Talking to people who have the empathy for you that you don't have for yourself helps to interrupt the dreadful rumination – I get so exhausted of the same thoughts going round and round my head. So a combination of the therapy with the self-group helped cut through that, which lifted me out of my depression.'

Counselling

A counsellor sees a client in a private and confidential setting to explore a difficulty the client is having, distress they may be experiencing or perhaps their dissatisfaction with life, or loss of direction and purpose.

This is the BACP's (British Association for Counselling and Psychotherapy - www.bacp.co.uk) description of counselling, the talking treatment that's most widely available in the UK. In this treatment, your counsellor listens carefully to what you have to say in order to get an idea of your life and the issues you are struggling with from your own perspective. A big part of a counsellor's job is being empathetic towards their clients. The aim is to help you see your difficulties from a different perspective (this is known as reframing), while providing an unbiased, non-judgemental and safe space for you to talk about the things that are bothering you.

Many people also find counselling helpful when it comes to venting repressed feelings like fear, embarrassment, grief or anger - feelings which you might not be comfortable discussing with other people in your life. There are a number of different types of counselling, including psychodynamic, behavioural, cognitive or humanistic (more information on this is available on the BACP website). The type your counsellor provides will depend on their theoretical perspective.

If you are referred to a counsellor by your GP, you will be offered anywhere up to six sessions. However, if you choose to see a counsellor privately, this timeframe will be much more flexible and you will be able to decide after a number of sessions whether you want or need any more. One important thing to note is that many experts feel that simply sitting and discussing your feelings is not always the best treatment to help clients with bipolar disorder. If you do decide counselling is the right talking treatment for you, ensure that the counsellor you talk to is properly trained and qualified to treat bipolar patients and their specific issues. Make sure that your therapist is aware of any risks and special considerations that your condition involves.

As a general rule, mood monitoring, learning to control destructive or negative behaviours and thoughts, and psycho-education should all play important roles in any talking treatment you receive.

Family-focused therapy

The third talking treatment that may be discussed when treating bipolar is family-focused therapy (FFT). This treatment combines two types of psychotherapy: family therapy and psycho-education (teaching patients and family members about the nature of the illness). As the name may suggest, this type of therapy is different from a lot of other forms as it focuses specifically on relationships and family dynamics, and how these factors can impact your condition. Some experts refer to family therapies as 'ecological therapies', as they tie patients and their conditions in with their families and surroundings, recognising that these cannot be considered as entirely separate.

Therapists specialising in FFT generally work towards identifying the tensions and difficulties that may exist within a family unit, and which may be contributing to stresses felt by patients and those around them. The term 'expressed emotion', referring to aggressive, over-involved or critical behaviours and attitudes expressed towards a family member with a psychiatric disorder, is often used in FFT sessions. For example, parents of someone with a condition like bipolar disorder may be upset about this illness, causing them to become overbearing or over-protective. This may then cause additional tension if/when the child rebels against this control. A key part of family-focused therapy involves becoming aware of these actions and reactions, and bringing them under control.

Psycho-education, the second part of FFT, works towards creating an understanding in the family for the nature of the condition, how it is treated and how a family member might go about being more supportive of their relative. This education can come in the form of handouts, training, assistance and lectures with a focus on problem-solving and communication.

Owing to the unpredictable and impulsive behaviours associated with bipolar, as well as the increased likelihood of suicidal tendencies, the condition can be incredibly demanding for anyone close to the patient. No matter how much a family member loves their relative with bipolar disorder, it is easy to get burned out and struggle to give the support that is needed. Importantly, a major focus of

FFT is on supporting the family members of people with conditions like bipolar. In many cases, it is in incredibly powerful tool for maintaining and creating a stable, healthy family unit.

Interpersonal and social rhythm therapy

Another form of talking treatment used for bipolar is interpersonal and social rhythm therapy (IPSRT). This treatment revolves around the understanding that bipolar is essentially a disturbance in your body-rhythm (things like seasonal rhythms, work-related/social rhythms and circadian rhythms) and that these disturbances can go on to alter your mood.

As we discussed in Chapter Three (What Causes Bipolar Disorder?), sleep deprivation often acts as a trigger for mania. IPSRT therapists aim to solve this problem by helping you introduce and maintain healthier sleep routines. As your sleep cycles become more regular, it is common for other disturbances in your body-rhythm to improve also. These rhythms are then tracked on a mood chart by the IPSRT therapist and their client along with daily activities and emotions, as in CBT.

In interpersonal and social rhythm therapy, you will be expected to keep a record of when you sleep, take medication, exercise, shop, eat, etc, as well as any social interactions which impact your mood and rhythms, such as interpersonal conflicts. The mood chart that is drawn up from this information is an important tool in improving your understanding of the relationship between your body and your mood. Some patients with bipolar find it to be a helpful tool in preventing mood swings.

Accessing talking therapies

As we discussed in Chapter 1, in order to access talking therapies through the NHS, you need to first talk to your GP. If they believe you would benefit from a talking therapy, they'll refer you to a therapist trained in family-focused therapy, CBT or counselling, such as a nurse, psychiatrist, social worker or psychologist.

Treatment with the NHS can be relatively hit-and-miss, and often the quality of treatment you receive will depend on where you live, with certain areas receiving better services than others. For this reason, if you can afford it, it can be a good idea to consider looking into private treatment.

Online/other resources

There are currently an immense number of self-help books on the market, which you will find in the book list later in this text. There are also countless websites online which deal with psychology and self-help. While some of these online resources should be avoided, certain services such as online forums have been found incredibly helpful by many people with bipolar, as they have provided the option of sharing stories with, and getting support from, other members of the bipolar community.

There are also two computer-based programmes provided by the NHS, which can currently be accessed by those living in Wales and England. 'Beating the Blues' aims to help people living with mild/moderate depression, while 'Fear Fighter' is for those with panic attacks or phobias. Although neither of these programmes were designed with people with bipolar in mind, they may be helpful in treating symptoms during manic or depressive episodes.

Importantly, before you try using these programmes, you should check with your mental health team to ensure they won't have a negative effect on your condition.

Summing Up

A great amount of evidence suggests that the most effective way to treat bipolar is through a combination of medication and talking therapy. One study, for example, found that those with bipolar often recovered more quickly from depressive episodes and were less likely to relapse when treated with both medication and intensive psychology than those who only received medication and a brief education on the illness.

Often the most helpful talking therapy for those with bipolar disorder is CBT - cognitive behavioural therapy. This is a type of therapy which aims to break down overwhelming problems into more acceptable, smaller parts. CBT is based on the core belief that that your thoughts impact the way you feel and act. By learning to avoid and identify destructive or otherwise negative ways of thinking, the individual can begin to avoid damaging behaviours and feel better.

Another important feature of CBT is learning to moderate your moods. The patient learns to notice early warning signs of depression and mania, and to get help in order to prevent these symptoms from evolving into a full-blown manic or depressive episode. CBT also teaches that the mood swings you experience are not necessarily bad things, and aims to help you accept them by normalising everyday highs and lows.

You may also find other talking therapies such as counselling, interpersonal and social rhythm therapy or family-focused therapy useful in treating bipolar disorder. These treatments are all available through the NHS and privately, but it's important that you make sure your therapist is fully trained, informed and skilled in treating bipolar disorder. Simply talking about your worries is not as effective as properly provided mood management or psycho-education.

Some treatments are available online, especially to those in England and Wales who can access CBT through NHS programmes like 'Beating the Blues' and 'Fear Fighter'. However, it's important that you check with your mental health team or GP that the programmes are right for you before beginning them.

Glossary of Terms

Acute
A disease with a rapid onset and short course (as opposed to chronic).

Antidepressant
A drug prescribed to relieve the symptoms of depression.

Antipsychotic
A drug prescribed to alleviate psychosis, mania and hypomania.

Bipolar disorder
A mental illness characterised by mood swings.

CAMHS (child and adolescent mental health)
Health services for children and young people under the age of 18.

Care plan
A series of action points chosen and written down by the person with bipolar disorder and their support team, which plan for their future care.

Carer
A person who cares for a sick or elderly person.

CBT (cognitive behavioural therapy)
A talking therapy that aims to modify the unhelpful thoughts and beliefs which cause dysfunctional emotions and behaviours.

Chronic
A persistent and lasting disease or medical condition (as opposed to acute).

Circadian clock
Another name for the body clock that controls our sleep-wake cycle, eating habits, body temperature and hormone secretion.

Community Mental Health Team (CMHT)
Commonly includes a psychiatrist, community psychiatric nurse (CPN), social worker, occupational therapist (OT), clinical psychologist and pharmacist.

Counselling
A form of talking therapy that provides a safe, confidential space for clients to discuss difficulties they may be having or distress they may be experiencing.

CPA (Care Programme Approach)
A care plan designed for someone who has been in hospital. Helps ease their transition back to life outside the hospital.

CPN (Community Psychiatric Nurse)
Nurses who support those with mental illnesses when they are not in hospital.

Crisis Resolution Team (CRT)
Provides 24-hour support for anyone experiencing a mental health crisis.

Cyclothymia
When manic or depressive symptoms last for two years or more, but are not serious enough for a diagnosis of bipolar disorder.

Depression
A persistent low mood, loss of energy and pleasure in previously enjoyable activities.

Diagnostic and Statistical Manual of Mental Disorders (DSM IV)
The fourth edition of a manual published by the American Psychiatric Association. Used in both the UK and US for categorising and diagnosing mental health problems.

Dopamine
A neurotransmitter that transmits signals between nerve cells and is part of the 'reward system', inducing pleasurable sensations in the brain.

Dual diagnosis
When a diagnosis such as bipolar disorder is accompanied by another clinical condition, such as drug addiction.

Family-focused therapy (FFT)
A form of talking treatment which combines psycho-education (teaching patients and their families about the nature of their illness) with a variety of family therapy.

GP (general practitioner)
A family doctor who treats people in the community.

Grandiosity
Delusions of power or superiority.

Hallucination
Seeing, smelling or hearing an object, person or experience that is not actually present.

Holding power
A legal process that allows a doctor to detain and assess a patient in hospital for 72 hours while they decide whether an application for a section needs to be made. A psychiatric nurse can exercise a holding power for up to six hours until a doctor can begin the assessment.

Holistic
Treating all aspects of the person, including their mind, emotions and body, not just the symptoms of their illness.

Hypomania
A persistent mild elevation of mood.

Hypothyroidism
A condition in which the thyroid gland doesn't produce enough of the hormone thyroxine.

Informal patient
Anyone who admits themselves to a psychiatric hospital voluntarily.

Insomnia
Persistent problems with sleep.

Interpersonal and social rhythm therapy
A form of talking therapy based on the idea that bipolar disorders are essentially body-rhythm disturbances.

Lithium
A medicine used to treat mood disorders such as severe depression or bipolar disorder.

Mania
An unnaturally high, euphoric mood.

Manic depression
The former name of bipolar disorder.

Mixed state
When symptoms of mania and depression occur at the same time.

Mood disorder
A mental illness, such as bipolar disorder, in which a disturbance with the person's mood is the main underlying feature.

Nearest relative
A patient's closest family member, who has certain rights.

Neurotransmitters
Chemicals that relay nerve impulses between brain and body.

NICE (National Institute for Clinical Excellence)
An independent organisation responsible for providing national guidance on the promotion of good health and the prevention/treatment of ill health in the UK.

Occupational therapy
The assessment and treatment of physical and psychiatric conditions using specific activities to improve all aspects of daily life.

OTC (over the counter)
Medicines that can be bought at any pharmacy without a prescription.

Paranoia
Delusional thinking in which someone feels persecuted.

Personality disorder
A mental illness characterised by a severe disturbance of someone's character, logic and behaviour.

Psychiatrist
A doctor specialising in mental illness.

Psycho-education
Teaches patients and their families about the nature of their illness.

Psychologist
A person qualified to study the human mind and treat mental illness.

Psychosis
A loss of contact with external reality.

Puerperal psychosis
A condition where symptoms of confusion, hallucinations and a loss of reality happen suddenly, often after childbirth.

Rapid cycling
Experiencing more than four mood swings in one year.

RORB gene
One of the 'clock genes' that controls our circadian clock. Scientists believe that an alteration in this gene is associated with bipolar disorder.

Schizoaffective disorder
A diagnosis that is used when someone does not have either typical schizophrenia or a typical mood disorder.

Schizophrenia
A mental illness involving psychological symptoms such as hallucinations, delusions and changes in behaviour.

Seasonal affective disorder (SAD)
A type of seasonal depression thought to be caused by a lack of sunlight in the winter months.

Section
Compulsory admittance to a psychiatric hospital or ward.

Serotonin
A neurotransmitter known as the brain's 'happy chemical'.

SNRIs (serotonin-norepinephrine reuptake inhibitors)
A class of antidepressant including Effexor and Cymbalta.

SSRIs (selective serotonin reuptake inhibitors)
A class of antidepressant including Prozac and Seroxat.

Talking therapy
Treating mental health problems using a therapy like counselling or CBT, either instead of or in-conjunction with medication.

Tricyclic
An older class of antidepressant largely replaced by SNRIs and SSRIs.

Ultra rapid cycling
When someone experiences monthly, weekly or even daily mood swings.

Unipolar
Describes depression where only low mood is experienced.

Withdrawal symptoms
The unpleasant physical and emotional reaction that occurs when an addictive substance is no longer taken.

Help list

Resources

Alcoholics Anonymous
Tel: 0845 769 7555 (helpline)
www.alcoholics-anonymous.org.uk
An informal society of millions of recovered alcoholics worldwide who follow a 12-step programme to become sober and remain so. AA meetings are available across the UK.

Bipolar4all
www.bipolar4all.co.uk
Describes itself as 'A safe haven for anyone touched by bipolar disorder'. Provides information on bipolar disorder, treatments and support – including the busy Bipolar4all forum.

British Association for Anger Management (BAAM)
Tel: 0845 1300 286
www.angermanage.co.uk
BAAM is the UK's leading organisation for all aspects of anger and conflict management. It runs evening and weekend courses, and has a wide range of resources and information on its website.

British Association for Behavioural and Cognitive Psychotherapies (BABCP)
Victoria Buildings, 9-13 Silver Street, Bury BL9 0EU
Tel: 0161 797 2670
www.babcp.com
BABCP is the leading organisation for cognitive behavioural therapy (CBT) in the UK and can help people find therapists in their local area.

British Association for Counselling and Psychotherapy (BACP)

BACP House, 15 St John's Business Park, Lutterworth LE17 4HB

Tel: 01455 883 316

bacp@bacp.co.uk

www.bacp.co.uk

The umbrella organisation for counselling in the UK. It should be your first port of call if you are looking to see a counsellor privately.

Centre for Stress Management

PO Box 26583, London SE3 7EZ

Tel: 020 7318 4448

www.managingstress.com

Runs cognitive-behavioural training programmes and offers exccutive, business, performance, stress and life coaching.

Depression Alliance

Depression Alliance, 20 Great Dover Street, London SE1 4LX

Tel: 0845 123 23 20

information@depressionalliance.org

www.depressionalliance.org

Working to relieve and prevent depression by providing information and support services to those who are affected by it via publications, supporter services and a network of self-help groups for people affected by depression.

eHealth Forum

http://ehealthforum.com/health/bipolar_disorder.html

Health community featuring member and doctor discussions ranging from a specific symptom to related conditions, treatment options, medication, side effects, diet and emotional issues surrounding bipolar disorder.

Institute for Complementary and Natural Medicine (ICNM)

Can-Mezzanine, 32-36 Loman Street, London SE1 0EH

Tel: 020 7922 7980

www.i-c-m.org.uk

Providing information on a wide range of complementary therapies and access to a register of qualified complementary therapists across the UK.

Institute of Family Therapy

24-32 Stephenson Way, London NW1 2HX

Tel: 020 7391 9150

www.instituteoffamilytherapy.org.uk

Providing counselling, therapy and mediation for families needing help.

MDF: the BiPolar Organisation

Castle Works, 21 St George's Road, London SE1 6ES

Tel: 020 7793 2600 (to become a member)

mdf@mdf.org.uk

www.mdf.org.uk

National user-led organisation and registered charity for people whose lives are affected by bipolar disorder. It aims to enable people affected by bipolar disorder to take control of their lives through a wide range of services, advice and support.

MIND

15-19 Broadway, Stratford, London E15 4BQ

Tel: 0045 700 0163 (helpline, Monday to Friday, 9am-5pm)

www.mind.org.uk

Providing information and advice to help people take control of their mental health.

Moodscope

www.moodscope.com

Free online mood-monitoring system, allowing you to keep a daily mood score and then record that on a chart plotting your moods over weeks and months. Invaluable tool for keeping track of your moods, then using that information for self-care and with your therapist and/or psychiatrist.

National Debtline

Tel: 0808 808 4000 (helpline, Monday to Friday 9am-9pm and Saturday 9.30am-1pm)

www.nationaldebtline.co.uk

Helpline providing free, confidential and independent advice on dealing with debt problems. Their advice is tailored to people living in different parts of the UK, because the law concerning debt is different in England, Wales and Scotland.

NHS Direct

Tel: 0845 4647 (helpline, Monday to Sunday, 24 hours)

www.nhsdirect.nhs.uk

Providing expert health advice, information and reassurance through a helpline and website.

Pendulum

www.pendulum.org

Extensive online resource on every aspect of bipolar disorder.

Relate

Premier House, Carolina Court, Lakeside, Doncaster DN4 5RA

Tel: 0300 100 1234

www.relate.org.uk

Charity offering advice, support, relationship counselling, sex therapy, workshops, mediation, consultations and support. You can either meet with a counsellor face to face, by phone or through their website.

Rethink

89 Albert Embankment, London SE1 7TP

Tel: 0845 456 0455 (helpline)

www.rethink.org

The leading national mental health membership charity working to help everyone affected by severe mental illness recover a better quality of life.

Royal College of Psychiatrists

17 Belgrave Square, London SW1X 8PG

Tel: 020 7235 2351

www.rpsych.ac.uk

The professional and educational body for psychiatrists in the United Kingdom and the Republic of Ireland. Its website provides an extensive resource on every aspect of mental health and wellbeing.

Samaritans

Chris, PO Box 9090, Stirling, FK8 2SA

Tel: 08457 90 90 90 (helpline, Monday to Sunday, 24-hour)

Tel: 1850 60 90 90 (helpline, Monday to Sunday, 24-hour, Republic of Ireland)

jo@samaritans.org

www.samaritans.org

Samaritans provides confidential, non-judgemental emotional support 24 hours a day for people who are experiencing feelings of distress or despair, including those which could lead to suicide.

SANE

1st Floor, Cityside House, 40 Adler Street, London E1 1EE

Tel: 0845 767 8000 (helpline, Monday to Sunday, 6pm-11pm)

sanemail@sane.org.uk

www.sane.org.uk

SANE is most famous for its national telephone line, which helps over 2,000 men, women and children every month who are affected by mental health issues.

Thyromind

www.thyromind.info

Information about thyroid disorders and the importance of thyroid function tests as part of the assessment of a mental health problem.

UK Narcotics Anonymous

Tel: 0300 999 1212 (helpline)

www.ukna.org

An informal society of millions of recovered drug addicts worldwide who follow a 12-step programme to free themselves from addiction. NA meetings are available across the UK.

United Kingdom Council for Psychotherapy (UKCP)

2nd Floor, Edward House, 2 Wakeley Street, London EC1V 7LT

Tel: 020 7014 9955

info@ukcp.org.uk

www.psychotherapy.org.uk

Umbrella organisation for psychotherapy in the UK. It should be your first port of call if you are looking to see a psychotherapist privately.

Book List

Mike Fisher, *Beating Anger: The Eight-Point Plan for Coping With Rage*, Random House, London, 2005

Paul Gilbert, *Overcoming Depression: A Self-Help Guide Using Cognitive Behavioral Techniques*, Constable & Robinson, London, 1997

Dr Liz Miller, *Mood Mapping: Plot Your Way to Emotional Health and Happiness*, Pan Macmillan, London, 2009

Sarah Owen and Amanda Saunders, *Bipolar Disorder: The Ultimate Guide*, Oneworld, Oxford, 2008

Jane Plant and Janet Stephenson, *Beating Stress, Anxiety and Depression: Groundbreaking Ways to Help You Feel Better*, Piatkus, London, 2008

Dorothy Rowe, *Depression: The Way Out of Your Prison*, Routledge, New York, 1983

Robert M Sapolsky, *Why Zebras Don't Get Ulcers: The Acclaimed Guide to Stress, Stress-Related Diseases and Coping*, Holt Paperbacks, New York, 2004

Jan Scott, *Overcoming Mood Swings: A Self-Help Guide Using Cognitive Behavioral Techniques*, Constable & Robinson, London, 2001

Jeremy Thomas and Dr Tony Hughes, *The A-Z Guide to Good Mental Health: You Don't Need to be Famous to Have Manic Depression*, Penguin, London, 2008

Reports, studies and leaflets

Bipolar Disorder (Manic Depression) leaflet, Royal College of Psychiatrists (available from www.rcpsych.ac.uk)

Cognitive Behavioural Therapy (CBT) leaflet, Royal College of Psychiatrists (available from www.rcpsych.ac.uk)

David Miklowitz, Psychosocial Treatments for Bipolar Depression, University of Colorado, published in the April 2007 issue of the journal Archives of General Psychiatry

MIND, In the Red: Debt and Mental Health, 2008

need2know

National Institute for Health and Clinical Excellence (NICE) (2005) CG38. Bipolar disorder: the management of bipolar disorder in adults, children and adolescents, in primary and secondary care.